BULLYING OF SIKH AMERICAN CHILDREN

THROUGH THE EYES OF A SIKH AMERICAN HIGH SCHOOL STUDENT

KARANVEER SINGH PANNU

Bullying of Sikh American Children

Library of Congress Control Number:
ISBN-13: 978-1519420138
ISBN-10: 1519420137

Contact us at:
Email: bullyingsikhamericanchildren@gmail.com
Website: www.bullyingsikhamericanchildren.org

LETTER OF APPRECIATION FROM PRESIDENT BARACK OBAMA

THE WHITE HOUSE

WASHINGTON

April 29, 2016

Karanveer Singh Pannu
Voorhees, New Jersey

Dear Karanveer:

Thank you for writing, and for sharing your story with me. Please know I admire your efforts to build a society without bullying.

Bullying is never okay, and I am committed to combating harassment and discrimination in our schools and communities. Each of us has a role to play in ensuring all Americans—no matter what they believe or where they come from—can feel safe to learn, grow, and work towards achieving their dreams, and I hope you take pride in your dedication to lifting up the lives of your fellow students.

Thank you, again, for your thoughtful message. I trust you will continue to raise your voice and use your talents to help America reach a brighter tomorrow, and I wish you all the best.

Sincerely,

TESTIMONIALS

Karanveer's book is a must read for educators who serve students from the Sikh community. The book provides the reader with an important description of the history of the Sikh people and provides details about the Sikh culture. The book is a great resource to help educators support Sikh students who are bullied frequently because people do not understand the Sikh culture and often because Sikhs wear a turban or head scarf. Many Sikh students are suffering on a daily basis and have the right, as all students have, to feel safe in school. Karanveer's book is a great resource for educators to help them create a safe school environment for Sikh students.

Dr. Diane Young, Assistant Superintendent.
Voorhees School District

Thank you for affording me the opportunity to read "Bullying of Sikh American Children". I learned a great deal and was enlightened by the history of Sikh faith. Your effort is commendable; hopefully providing insight and strategies will compel others to adjust perceptions surrounding the Sikh culture. Thank you for bringing attention to this matter in a compassionate and mature manner.

Bill Westerby, Vice Principal
Eastern Regional High School

The scope and depth of young Mr. Karnveer Singh Pannu's work offers new insight to even the most sensitive of educators and holds out hope to children who are bullied because of their memberships in a faith community. Bullying of Sikh American Children: Through the eyes of a Sikh American High School student offers a comprehensive array of chapters providing a resource for education about the Sikh faith and its practices, media and community portrayal of Sikhs, statistics about bullying and its psychological impact, and strategies for change. Particularly touching is Mr. Pannu's determination to improve conditions for his community from a place of strength; this gracious, kind, determined, intelligent young researcher and writer is wise beyond his years.

Susan M. Pomerantz, M.A., Teacher of English
Eastern Regional High School

As an educator, I do my best to get to know each of my students and connect with them on a level beyond classroom learning. I have had the opportunity and pleasure of having Karanveer Singh enroll in my Business Law course. During a casual conversation, the others in our class and myself learned of his endeavor of writing a book addressing bullying of Sikh Americans. He was generous enough to share his book with me, and I was eager to not only learn of the talents of one of my students, but also to learn more of the Sikh beliefs.

As I ready Bullying of Sikh American Children: Through the eyes of a Sikh American High School student, I realized just how ignorant I have been to those around me. I work in a very diverse school, yet knew very little of the students I taught that were of the Sikh faith. The more I learned, the more I realized how little I knew, and this was a very humbling experience. Since my exposure to this easy to understand and informative book, I have become aware of the students that walk our halls, those that live in my neighborhood, as well as issues that people that embrace the Sikh faith encounter in their lives outside of school.

Reading Karanveer's book has created much awareness within me that I can share with other students as well as my own family. Acceptance through understanding is one of the greatest lessons life can offer and I am filled with admiration of Karanveer for addressing issues that are simply ignored. No words can truly reflect how much his book impacted my way of thinking and how I view so many around me. Congratulations to this young man for his tremendous accomplishment. I have no doubt he will continue his successful journey in any avenue he chooses to pursue. Many of us can learn a number of life's lessons from his accomplishment.

Audrey Pappas
Eastern Regional High School

DEDICATION

This book is dedicated to my exceptional grandmother Kirat Rajpal Singh. In memory of my grandfather Rajpal Singh and my uncle Dr. Vikram Singh, both of whom I never knew but deeply cherish the stories about their incredibly fulfilling lives. To my uncle Ramneek Singh, who has been my inspiration and role model because of all the wonderful social causes he continues to work for, all due to his genuine empathy for the environment, animals, and humans alike. No words can suffice to thank my mother, Amrita, for giving her unconditional love and support.

TABLE OF CONTENTS

ACKNOWLEDGEMENTS

This project has had many contributors, but the key to motivating me to bring out this book has been my father. His ever-persistent prodding and support has kept me going to complete this endeavor. I cannot thank my father enough for the umpteen critiques and editing he helped with 'til I got it right. My mother, whose selfless love, discipline, and fortitude has been unbelievable. My smart younger brother Sherveer's incisive brain always has something good to contribute, add value, and to get to the kernel quickly.

Thanks to the many aunts, uncles, relatives, and friends who did not hesitate to give candid suggestions, their valuable time, and hard-earned funds to support this project. There are not enough words to thank all of them for the gratitude I feel for their unwavering support in believing in my project and me. There are many kind and generous well-wishers of this book project. They all have one thing in common, i.e., genuine empathy for others around them and wanting to help by easing those problems which cause pain and suffering, especially to young growing children.

I would be remiss in my responsibility if I did not mention Uncle Mohinder Singh Kalsi and Uncle Kirpal Singh Nijher, who have played a pivotal role in persuading and inspiring me to push myself further.

Once again, my sincere thanks for sponsoring and supporting this much needed book by Dr. Baljinder Singh Dhillon, Rajvir Singh Dhillon, Dr. Navinderdeep Singh Nijher, Dr. Sukhbir Kaur Nijher, Dr. Navdeep Singh Nijher, Dr. Ardeep Kaur Sekhon, Dr. Ajay Partap Singh Bajwa, Dr. Harpreet Kaur Nijher, Dr. Methab Singh Bajwa, Mrs. Meenu Kaur Bajwa, Dr. Manohar Singh Grewal, Jasbir Kaur Bhullar, Dr. Mohandeep

Singh Dhillon, Dr. Shamsher Kaur Dhillon, Harvinder Singh Sran, Dr. Manbir Singh, Mohinder Singh Kalsi, Ishwar Singh, Dr. Harpal Singh Dhillon, Mrs. Surjit Kaur Dhillon, Gurvinder Singh Sandhu, Narinder Singh Bhasin, Iqbal Singh Chopra, Dibjot Singh, Akashdeep Singh Aujla, Dr. Gurdas Singh Dass, Dr. Surinder Singh Chauhan, Ajit Singh Walia, Yaspal Singh Bains, Manjit Kaur Bains, Inderpreet Singh, Guru Nanak Sikh Society of the Delaware Valley, Pine Hill, New Jersey, and Tejwant Singh Mangat and Gurvinderpal Singh Juneja of Colorado Singh Sabha, Commerce City, Colorado.

I want to thank Dr. Akashdeep Aujla, Dr. Kirpal Singh, Dr. Surinder Singh Sodhi, Dr. Kanwar Sidhu, Dr. Pal Singh Brar, Dr. Massi Shamilov, and Dr. Chiranjeet Kaur Brar, all child psychiatrists and psychologists, who gave their valuable time to be interviewed and giving their valuable suggestions.

My heartfelt thanks to those who spent hours going over my multiple drafts to give their wisdom and experienced input, especially Dr. Maureen Hogan, Dr. Ines Meier, Dr. Bill Whitlow, Dr. Robert Lee Edmonds, Dr. Diane Young, Kirpal Singh Nijher, Jasbir Kaur Bhullar, Mohinder Singh Kalsi, Ms. Mary Ann Walker, and Ms. Irene Afek.

Karanveer Singh Pannu
November 1, 2015

PREFACE

The intent of this book is to introduce the reader to the unique challenges Sikh American children face in their daily lives, both in and out of the school environment. In particular, children in the Sikh American community have been the targets of severe bullying. The entire Sikh faith collective has faced this ongoing problem of bullying through overt and covert means for over 100 years of its existence in America. However, bullying has increased markedly since 9/11. As a result, this issue been challenged and a few Sikh American advocacy organizations have been trying to deal with bullying in a methodical and systematic fashion.

Research on the bullying of Sikh children in America has been limited. Sikh American advocacy organizations, like the Sikh Coalition and SALDEF, have been instrumental in conducting research on bullying in schools and about the ignorance of the "turban." This data has been enlightening to educators, who can then start to build on the basic foundational work done by the organizations. Without hard data, it becomes difficult to quantify and make a case for assistance and support by the school administration, whether it be local, state, or at the national level.

By highlighting this very important issue through the eyes of a high school student like me, teachers, administrators, and the general public will be exposed to the challenges and possible solutions to make the schools everywhere a more conducive and productive place for learning rather than a place of everyday fear and anxiety for thousands of children like me across our great country.

Many ideas do not seem to get any traction because of the impasse of the school administration, teachers and others involved due to time constraints, laws which stymie practical common sense solutions, and the fear of frivolous lawsuits. Mental peace without non-educational stress for any school-going child is extremely important; only then can one concentrate on his/her studies wholeheartedly in order to excel. If a child is worried constantly about being bullied in any shape or form, it has a direct and strong negative effect on the learning process. Therefore, any and all innovative concepts and ideas should be used to best fulfill the needs of each child, their parents, and other supporting adults.

Changing attitudes of humans from preconceived positions takes time and effort. It requires major resources, and this has been a monumental hurdle for the Sikh American community in general. Since Sikhs do not have a clergy, centralized or otherwise, it has been up to the lay person to take up the task of educating and communicating to the general public about the Sikh faith, history, and the cultural heritage. As mentioned earlier, due to the lack of any centralized clergy, the content put together by various Sikh American organizations may vary in precise definitions. Overall, the general theme is the same in the literature being disseminated through brochures, booklets, websites, blogs, and smartphone apps.

More in-depth solutions to solve the bullying problem will take time, creativity, collective effort, financial resources, a long-term vision, change in some of the existing laws, and a lot of perseverance, only then will the status quo change. I am optimistic that nothing is insurmountable, and if the community rallies together, many of the existing concerns will be resolved eventually.

Sikh parents in particular must be cognizant of the fact that they do not have to cower and try to coerce their own children to physically assimilate; rather, they should have their children stay proudly distinguished by instilling many of the suggested solutions in this book in order to live with their heads held high and navigate school life with the life skill tools to deal with any kind of bullying in and out of school.

My fervent hope is that my peers, their parents, teachers, adminis-trators, legislators, local officials, counselors, psychiatrists, psychologists, and other specialists in the field of education and the general public will become aware and empathetic to the unique challenges faced every day by children of the Sikh faith as a result of this book.

I have used my own personal experience to suggest many practical and proactive in order to alleviate the level of bullying on Sikh American children. The proposed strategies require time, effort, and a balanced dose of common sense, but most of all, a commitment by the parents to train their young over a long timeline through personal leadership. There are no shortcuts to training so that children can face the daily challenges of the world.

As this book was going to press, a particularly promising national ini-tiative to target bullying of Sikh American children was announced by the White House. On October 15, 2015, a public awareness campaign, Act To Change, was introduced to address bullying in Sikh and Asian American communities.[1] The bullying campaign seeks to empower students, parents, teachers, and communities to report, stop, and prevent bullying.

---

[1] www.acttochange.org

INTRODUCTION OF THE AUTHOR

I have had the good fortune to know Karanveer and his family for a number of years. It takes everything you have as a parent to bring up a child in an environment where there are extremely few who look like you. I have seen Karanveer in his formative years as he has been regularly attending Camp Khanda, a week-long summer camp for Sikh children. My interaction with Karanveer has been somewhat more than other children since I have worked with his father on important Sikh issues for a long time and followed his various achievements. Starting in 2014, Karanveer has been nominated to be a Sikh youth counselor at the summer camp because he has shown excellent leadership skills with a strong foundation in his faith.

I have three children and seven grandchildren of my own and keenly understand all the issues laid out in this book. As my own children were growing up in a small town in upstate New York in the 70s and 80s, we had our own set of challenges as my children were the only kids of the Sikh faith in township and lived at least hundred miles away from the nearest city with any other visible Sikhs. Fortunately, my wife was a high school teacher and I was a professional engineer, so we had the foresight to be able to tackle many issues proactively in order to make the academic environment within the school conducive to learning rather than a place of anxiety due to bullying. With tremendous effort and the Almighty's grace, all my kids pulled through to become physicians, good practicing Sikhs, and phenomenal Americans. Both my sons were Eagle Scouts. My older son, Dr. Navinderdeep Singh Nijher, was one of the first ER interns to volunteer at Ground Zero during the immediate aftermath of the terrible

9/11. Even he was bullied by other adults at Ground Zero while he gave everything he had trying to save others selflessly.

So, I truly understand the need for this book. If I had this book when my children were growing up, I am convinced that many more Sikh children would have had the tools to tackle bullying and learnt ways to deal with it more effectively and most definitely improving any chances of long-term trauma caused by bullying.

I cannot thank Karanveer enough to bring out this ground-breaking, solution-oriented book, which should be a must-read by children starting from middle school to high school, parents, teachers, counselors, bullying specialists, administrators, legislators, and the general public. If everyone who is involved, i.e., the bullied and the bully, acquired something positive from this book, the school would be a far better place for learning because that is the primary reason children go there.

I want to congratulate Karanveer for the outstanding work he has done to bring out this fantastic book in order to help his peers and thousands of others who suffer from bullying daily.

Kirpal Singh Nijher, BS (Eng.), MBA
Founding Member – Global Sikh Council
Past Chair – American Sikh Council
Current member – Boy Scouts Task Force (American Sikh Council)
www.americansikhcouncil.org
Director – Camp Khanda
www.campkhanda.org

INTRODUCTION

I have thought long and hard about how I can help fix bullying, which for Sikh American children is a constant stress subconsciously and is a daily reality. So, I decided to walk the walk and talk the talk, just like my father has taught and shown me.

I have always been very cognizant of my attire and the reaction of "others" to me. The questions, the stares, the passing whispers, the snickering, the audible taunts from the invisible voice from the crowd, and much more, which is something normal for every visible Sikh American child or adult. No wonder anyone like me has to grow a thicker skin than others in order to survive.

A few years ago as a freshman, I realized based on my observations how children interacted inside the hallways of my high school. The change from middle school was dramatic and different. In middle school, children are still immature and bullying is more straightforward and physical. In high school, the bullying is more subtle, which includes texting, use of the Internet, and because of that, it can become violent and the threats more serious. I realized that bullying is overt and also covert. The issue of bullying is multidimensional since it is primarily a power play of domination by one or by a few over another individual.

My personal bullying experiences have been minimal and not too serious, all thanks to my parents' foresight and proactive training. I was fortunate to have the resources which other children possibly did not. Not everyone is so fortunate to have vigilant parents, a cooperative school administration, and supportive friends, all to create an overall conducive environment to minimize bullying in and out of school.

Statistics show that the bullying against Sikh American children are nearly double the national average within the US. These very daunting numbers is what got me thinking as to how I could help empower my peers and others in order to try to stop the spread of the insidious "bullying virus" so that no child in America should go through this kind of trauma.

Since this book is about the bullying of Sikh American children, the reader needs to know that there are some challenges which are unique to them, yet other issues are common to all children. This interplay and overlay of issues can only be understood in the proper context if there is a descriptive background of the affected children's faith and history. The role of Sikh American adults has to be explained in order for the reader to understand some background and the overall related issues.

Therefore, after identify the "Challenges for Sikh Children" in the first chapter, the next chapter covers the brief background of the fundamentals of "The Sikh Faith." Since the distinguished Sikh turban is so emotive to most of the general public, it has been dealt in a separate chapter to clarify its significance. The chapter on "Sikhs in America" is again a brief history covering the early period of the last century and the ongoing trials and tribulations of the Sikh immigrants dealing with bullying.

In order to understand others, it is important that a person understands his/her own background first; therefore, the chapter on "Christianity, Judaism, Eurocentrism, and the Blind Spot" is vital as it lays out the absurdity of the "turban question" in the minds of most Americans. The chapter on "Post-9/11: Adult to Children Trickle-Down Effect" goes over the psychological fear of the unknown other and its effects. The chapter on "Media Portrayal of the Sikhs" covers how big-screen cinema, from Hollywood to Bollywood, the general media, video games, etc., ignorantly denigrate turbans and beards, aiding in more bullying of Sikh Americans.

In order to understand the ground reality, I decided to conduct my own personal bullying survey with some very interesting results in the chapter on

"Current Bullying Statistics for Sikh American Children." In the subsequent chapter, I covered "Psychological Trauma: Interviews with Mental-Health Professionals," where I have given a few examples of severe bullying of Sikh American children and then my personal interviews with several child psychiatrists, covering the effects and possible solutions for bullying.

Finally, I have written the last two chapters covering various strategies. In the chapter on "Strategies for Families," I have shared my personal experiences and the numerous ideas which I proactively used to insulate myself from the effects of bullying. The last chapter is on "Strategies for Educators," which covers all the possible ways teachers, administrators, legislators, and other outside agencies can do to dissipate bullying.

It is very hard to understand what it feels to be in someone else's shoes. The only way to understand is to live it, but that is not practical, as we all know. Since I have personally lived and experienced the life of a student from kindergarten to 11th grade through the public school system while dealing with the issue of bullying, I am in a position to give real, practical, workable solutions which can possibly make the difference for a bullied child between ongoing misery and a fulfilling childhood in school.

CHALLENGES OF BULLYING FOR SIKH CHILDREN

"Courage is fire, and bullying is smoke."
Benjamin Disraeli [2]

WHAT IS BULLYING?

According to the Stop Bullying initiative, "Bullying is unwanted, aggressive behavior among school aged children that involves a real or perceived power imbalance. The behavior is repeated, or has the potential to be repeated, over time. Both kids who are bullied and who bully others may have serious, lasting problems."[3]

When the strong preys on the weak, when the powerful preys on the powerless, when the popular person preys on the unpopular, and it is unwanted, repetitive aggressive behavior which makes the bullied victim feel threatened to become an emotional wreck.

Bullying occurs when the bully tries to intimidate, harass, or tyrannize the victim to cower, oppress, and dominate.[4] While the bully feels powerful and empowered in an evil sort of way, the victim is fearful, filled with anxiety, and becomes depressed, eventually causing other problems.[5]

---

[2] http://www.brainyquote.com/quotes/keywords/bullying.html#GbE7FAx8oWECJbxO.99

[3] http://www.stopbullying.gov/what-is-bullying/definition/index.html

[4] http://www.stopbullying.gov/what-is-bullying/definition/

[5] http://www.eyesonbullying.org/victim.html

There are myriad forms of bullying, from adult to children, based on race, color, ethnicity, religion, and much more. In my experience, there are two large categories of bullying. One is bullying based on lack of knowledge. The other is bullying by design. The bully is knowledgeable and knows exactly why he/she is bullying.

The premise of the book is to cover both categories of bullying. I suggest a large part of the bullying of Sikh American children in schools can be improved with more comprehensive education on world history, geography, social studies covering religion, with emphasis on Asia, Africa, and the Middle East, which, at the moment, is lacking.

THE CASE OF SIKH AMERICAN CHILDREN

Children of the Sikh faith have always had challenges, sometimes unique but most times the same which any distinguished minority faith, ethnic group, or people of color have to deal with regularly.

I have heard so many stories from my father getting bullied when he was in school being the only child of the Sikh faith in a school of over a thousand kids. These bullying issues have always remained in schools since schools came into existence. The difference being that during the 60s to 80s when my father was in school, there was no one to help him against bullying as it was not taken as seriously like it is today by school authorities. During his time, one was left to defend with wits and fists. If neither was available, it was tough luck. The strong survived and weak gave up, and a very important distinguishing article of faith, the "long uncut hair covered in a turban," simply disappeared, and the kid would more than likely break away from his religion as a means of stopping the unremitting verbal and physical attacks, which often ended up being traumatic.

There have been some changes for the better, while other issues have still remained.

When one is distinguished, you stand out in a crowd, and no matter how strong you are, it is easy for someone to pass an insulting remark, and it is hard if one is unable to even react because either the rest join in or it is a nameless voice from the crowd. The same scenario, if escalated, can have all kinds of repercussions where invariably the victim will end up getting into trouble and not the perpetrator, especially if there is a physical reaction from the victim.

There are many examples of the victim being mistreated by the school authorities. Many times a child has been repeatedly bullied, complained to the authorities, yet minimal action has been taken. If the Sikh child does not get help or reacts on his/her own, eventually the humiliation and anger will build up to spew out at some point. Instead of the school authorities being taken to task for not doing their part, the victim is suspended. This situation has happened to thousands of Sikh students over many decades. In recent years, due to organizations like the American Sikh Council, Sikh Coalition, SALDEF, United Sikhs, there has been some pressure put on the school systems to provide a safer environment for Sikh children.

The HIB Act (Harassment, Intimidation & Bullying) has been implemented in schools, which evidently are helping eliminate most of the physical bullying, but it has not stopped the common verbal diatribe which occurs during school recess, homerooms, hallways, cafeterias, restrooms, etc. Laws must change in our nation to protect everyone from all forms of bullying, and that means even the tiniest communities, such as the Native American groups.

Sikh American–led organizations are doing their part by providing aid through the legislative system, but the brunt of the "Sikh Bullying Dilemma" can be alleviated to a large extent right in the homes of Sikh children! The solution lies in the way Sikh parents raise their children. I believe once parents realize that their children look up to them as role models and emulate their lives, there will be a change for the better. Therefore, it behooves every right-thinking, concerned parents to become upstanding citizens and lead ethical lives which show their own children that they are not cowardly hypocrites but truly believe and follow the principles of their faith as honest and strong individuals. This planned change in the lives of adults can positively alter the lives of their own children to arm themselves with all the tools and skills to defend themselves against many bullying issues to a large extent, even though they can never be completely eliminated from society.

In order for everyone to understand the unique challenges facing Sikh American children, I have first covered and explained in a brief overview of "The Sikh Faith," a short history of the "Turban," and an account of "Sikhs in America" in the following chapters.

THE SIKH FAITH

INTRODUCTION

Out of the seven major faiths—namely, Christianity, Islam, Judaism—these three originate from the Middle East, while the other four—Buddhism, Jainism, Hinduism and the Sikh faith—originate from the Asian continent. The Sikh faith is strictly a monotheistic religion and over 545 years old. It is the 5th largest faith in the world with between 28–30 million followers across the globe.

WHO IS A SIKH?

The Sikh religion originated in the Punjab region of South Asia located in the Northwest section of what is modern-day India and the Northeast section of modern Pakistan. Punjabi/Gurmukhi is the primary language of the Punjab region.

In the Punjabi language, the word "Sikh" means student or learner. The purpose of being a Sikh is to learn as much as possible from the *Guru Granth Sahib*, the Sikh religious scripture, has to offer in order for the Sikh to put those teachings to practice in order to become better human beings.

According to the Sikh code of conduct, the "Rehat Maryada," a Sikh is described as "one who professes the Sikh religion, believes and follows the teachings of Sri Guru Granth Sahib and the Ten Gurus only, and keeps unshorn hair and has no other religion."[6]

---

[6] Sikh Rehat Maryada, 1978 Dharam Parchar Committee, Shiromani Gurdwara Parbandhak Committee, Amritsar

The founding father of the Sikh religion was Guru Nanak. He is known as the first Guru of the Sikh faith. He was born in 1469 in Talwandi, Punjab. Guru Nanak was born into an upper caste Hindu family. He broke away from the grasp of the Brahmanical Hindu caste system.[7] At that time in history, the rigid caste system and arcane rituals took an enormous toll on the bulk of society because no individual could function—from birth to death, from opening a new business to buying a home and much more—without the paid services of a Brahmin. Anyone not using a Brahmin by paying him to send prayers to "god" was permanently shunned by society because of the inelastic religious system put in place by the same Brahmin Hindus.

Guru Nanak had a revelation in which he saw what it would take to get onto the right path and to achieve unity with God the Creator. The ideals and ways he began to practice during the time were practical, scientific, and simple. Consequently, many Muslims, Hindus, Jains, and Buddhists began to follow Guru Nanak. The word "Guru" literally means teacher.

True equality among humans, freedom of religion, freedom from (class) racism, freedom from tyranny, love of all humanity, stopping all meaningless rituals, liberty, and justice for all were some of the basic postulates which were strongly espoused and inculcated to all through his teachings.

Nine more Gurus solidified Guru Nanak's teachings through their own lives. The 10th and final living Guru, Guru Gobind Singh, passed away in 1708, leaving an uninterrupted legacy of 239 years of teaching. This is the longest legacy of any monotheistic faith where the Gurus themselves have taught, trained, and led their followers through an example of their personal lives in order for the newly formed faith to take root. Jesus Christ preached for barely three and half years before he left this earth.

Each Guru, during his lifetime, wrote down his beliefs, ideas, and principles in the form of poetry. All the writings of the Gurus who did write were completely in line with the founder Guru Nanak's ideals. These

---

[7] Brahmanism was organized into a "caste system," a self-perpetuating, multi-tiered socioeconomic apparatus. Society was divided into various degraded systems by the elite Brahmins, who are topmost caste, while at the very bottom are the untouchables.

writings were formalized into the *Adi Granth* in 1604 and later, in 1708, formalized and proclaimed as the *Guru Granth Sahib Ji*—the final Guru (scripture)—forever. The Guru Granth Sahib Ji contains the teachings of first five and the 9th Gurus.[8] The other Gurus did not have writings to be incorporated into the final scripture. There are writings of many other Muslim saints and Hindu bards all from various castes/lower classes whose writings were incorporated because they were very much in line with the Gurus' theological thought. The Guru Granth Sahib Ji is written in 1430 pages, all in poetry, which can be sung in meters (ra-ags) traditionally with stringed instruments.[9] Music has been used as a medium to convey the divine message of love and humanistic values to the Sikh congregations.

The holy scripture of the Sikhs is today available in almost any language and can be delivered online via G.O.D Co. (Guru Granth Sahib Ji on Demand).[10] The Sikh religion is the only faith today which has the writings directly written and authenticated by the original writers (the Sikh Gurus) during their lives, which is found in the Guru Granth Sahib Ji.[11]

The 10th Guru, Guru Gobind Singh Ji, bestowed the Guruship (the official mandate) to the Sikh Scripture before his passing away, and therefore, the Guru Granth Sahib Ji permanently and forever became the "Guru" in 1708. In other words, the scripture became the final Guru. The word "Guru" means teacher, the word "Granth" means a voluminous scripture, and the word "Sahib" denotes a temporal master. Interesting fact, the word "Guru," when split in two means, "Gu" - darkness and "Ru" - light. Essentially a Guru is one who breaks through darkness (ignorance) and replaces it with light (enlightenment).

---

[8] Six Gurus and writings of other Muslim and Hindu Saints were incorporated, but only those writings which stood the touchstone of the founder's Guru Nanak's ideal religious postulates.

[9] In addition to stringed instruments, the table and harmonium are commonly used, even though the harmonium was an insertion by the British to change the Sikh faith subtly. The Holy Scripture is available online today.

[10] www.sikh.net

[11] The "Kartarpuri Bir" is an authenticated Sikh scripture and an original copy is still available in the custody of the Sodhi family in the city of Kartarpur, Punjab.

It is very important to note that the Sikh faith is *not* a hybrid of Islam and Hinduism or a sect or a denomination of either. The Sikh faith is an independent revealed religion which stands by itself with very clear and distinct beliefs. There are common values which the Sikh faith shares with many other faiths. However, the Sikh faith is not a mixture of any other religion.

SIKH UNIFORM AND THE SIKH TURBAN

To help discipline the mind, promote equality, and break away from the existing Hindu caste system, the Sikh Gurus specified a uniform that every neophyte must wear to take the first step in order to get on the path of the Sikh faith. In the Sikh religion, this uniform mandates keeping the human body intact to its maximum extent just the way it was given to us by the Creator. In other words, would you take your brand new Lamborghini Aventador and spray paint it, take its paint off, or puncture its wheels? Pretty sure no one would dare touch a very pricy vehicle like that. Similarly, the Sikh faith believes that our bodies are priceless. Therefore, the Sikh Gurus have asked their followers to stop deforming or ruining their bodies through unnecessary rituals, cutting/shaving hair, or ritually cutting any part of the body, etc. To keep the hair neat and clean, each and every Sikh male is required to wear a turban, and it is optional for a woman. Though more and more women are choosing to wear it by choice. A turban functions as part of the Sikh uniform, just like the uniform of your local police officer or soldier. The turban indicates to anyone in distress that they can approach this individual for help without any fear or hesitation.

If you are a practicing Sikh, one who says he/she follows the Sikh religion, then he/she is mandated to maintain the five articles of faith in addition to respecting the four primary prohibitions.[12]

The 5 kakkars (articles of faith), or Ks, are as follows:
- Kesh: uncut hair,
- Kara: steel/iron bracelet signifying bond to God,

---

[12] As per the Sikh Rehait Maryada, the Sikh moral code of conduct.

20

- Kanga: wooden comb placed in hair to signify cleanliness,
- Kachera: long breeches (somewhat similar to those worn by Mormon Christians and the Hasidic Jews), and the
- Kirpan: sword of varying lengths there to defend the weak, the needy, and self.

Those who have committed to the faith or have gone through the formal "Kanda Da Phaul" initiation ceremony and taken the final step to become part of the fraternity of the Khalsa are required to wear these articles of faith. This process was to create a sense of discipline within the individual to follow a righteous path in order to become a great human being and help others.

The four primary prohibitions are as follows: do not cut your hair, do not eat Halal meat (meat that is undergone a ritualistic process),[13] do not commit adultery, and, most importantly, do not take any kind of intoxicants/drugs!

Sikh Gurus also asked their followers to stop distorting their bodies through the pointless rituals like circumcision, tattoos, piercing and/or cutting, or shaving of hair performed in many other faiths.

IMPORTANT SIKH BELIEFS

The Sikh faith believes in One Creator, equality of all men and women, right of freedom to profess any faith, right to self-defense to possess arms, life of honesty, humility and dignity, consider all humans as one family without divisions, life of a householder,[14] with freedom, liberty and justice for all.

Further, Sikhs do not believe in any kind of superstitions, rituals in the name of religion, idol worship, divisions based on color, gender, national origin, religion, caste or superiority.

---

[13] The Muslim Halal method.

[14] Unlike other faiths where people live austere single lives away from society rather than living in society and trying to live an honest, disciplined, ethical life while living in harmony with all.

CONCEPT OF THE CREATOR IN THE SIKH FAITH

The Sikh religion's beliefs are extremely modern, scientific, and devoid of constraints, like micromanaging a person's life. According to Sikh faith, hypocritical and/or dogmatic rituals have no meaning and are a waste of time and energy. The Sikh faith is a truly a monotheistic faith. Thus, with its belief in One Creator only and none else, the faith does not recognize anything or anybody else as equal to the Creator.

According to the fundamental concept of the Creator within the Sikh faith, the Creator is not subject to birth or death, has a measurable life span, a sense of hate, or fears anyone, and is always omnipresent.

SIKH MORALS AND ETHICS

The Sikh faith's fundamental principles are based on ethical conduct all the times, anywhere, and with anyone. Truth is a high moral characteristic in an individual, but the highest is truthful living, as espoused by the Sikh scripture, Shri Guru Granth Sahib Ji.

> Below the ultimate Truth are all the endeavors to be divine; wherein, the highest amongst such endeavors is the attainment of a Truthful Character.[15]

The three basic pillars and the ethical foundation of the Sikh faith are

- *Kirat Karo*: earn your living through completely honest means;
- *Wand Chako*: share your earnings with others by serving humanity through completely selfless service;
- *Naam Japo*: remember the Creator at all times in order to continuously stay focused upon morally ethical virtues to use in our daily lives.

---

[15] SGGS, Page 62

RELATIONSHIP WITH OTHER FAITHS

Though the Sikh religion shares some beliefs with Islam, Christianity, Judaism, as well as some schools of Hindu thought, it is distinct from them. According to Guru Nanak, the founder of the Sikh faith,

> I do not fast nor do I observe Ramadan, I only serve One God who always protects me. . . . I do not go on Hujj to Kaa'ba nor do I go on any pilgrimage. I serve only One and no other. . . . I am not a Hindu nor am I a Muslim.[16]

Tolerance toward other religions is an integral part of the faith. According to the Guru Nanak,

> Don't say the Vedas or the Books (scriptures of Islam, Christianity, and Judaism) are false. False is one who does not study (them).[17]

Guru Nanak teaches his followers to respect of all humans regardless of their faith:

> O Friend! I have totally forgotten my jealousy of others since I found the Company of the Guru, the Enlightener. Now, no one seems like an enemy, and no one is a stranger to me anymore. I get along with everyone. Now, whatever God does, I accept as good (for His creation.) This is the sublime wisdom I have obtained from the Guru. The One God is pervading in all. Gazing upon His creation and beholding Him present in everyone, Nanak blossoms forth in happiness.[18]

---

[16] SGGS, Page 243

[17] SGGS, Page 831

[18] SGGS, Page 1299

According to Sikh faith, misunderstandings can be removed by being in the company of virtuous people. The Sikh Gurus have highlighted this problem of divisions and provided a solution in the above commandment. Bullying is the antithesis of the Sikh faith and Guru Nanak's directive as well, in my personal experience. My father taught us to feel the Creator in every human heart and to look upon everyone as friends instead of strangers; therefore, bullying is not in my repertoire.

Historically, humans have made barriers amongst themselves based on race, color, gender, nationality, religion, caste, or culture, etc.

CONCEPT OF GURDWARA AND LANGAR

The Sikh house of prayer is known as a Gurdwara. Sikh Gurus made sure "all" are welcome at the Gurdwara, regardless of race, color, religion, gender, caste, etc. The most sacred Gurdwara, known as the Darbar Sahib[19] in Amritsar, Punjab, was built with open doors facing in all the four directions to symbolize that "Sikh Houses of Prayer" are open to all people coming from all the four directions of the globe. It is the only religious institution which has been built lower than the surroundings to convey humility. To further emphasize the idea of "equality of all," everyone in a "Sikh House of Prayer" sits on the floor with no special place, chair, or cushion assigned for anyone. There are no priests or clergy; therefore, any Sikh, regardless of age or gender, can perform the prayers in the congregation and/or read the Guru Granth Sahib.

Most Gurdwaras, the Sikh houses of prayer, operate the Guru's "langar"[20] (free community kitchen), which further emphasizes the idea of equality for all. Everyone sits and dines together sitting on the floor. The idea of sitting together on the floor to eat is to promote humility

---

[19] Darbar Sahib or Harmandar Sahib, which has been incorrectly labeled the Golden Temple by the British and everyone has continued to use it globally, even today. Imagine calling the Vatican the "white dome temple" or holiest Mosque at Mecca as the "black stone temple"?

[20] The free community kitchen is traditionally called a Guru's "langar" with respect as it further emphasizes equality for all.

and erase all class distinctions by promoting fraternity of all. Even today, in many parts of South Asia and particularly in India, food is still used as way to discriminate against others, particularly among the upper caste Hindus.[21] Anyone visiting a Gurdwara is free to volunteer in the preparation and distribution of the Guru's langar. Through the process of preparing food for others and selflessly distributing the food, the sense of service to humanity, "Sewa,"[22] is instilled in everyone who participates and eats in the Guru's langar. The Sikh faith is probably the only faith which has free community dining as an integral part of their prayer services.

A recent example of magnanimous nature of the Sikh faith occurred when the American Sikh Council led a contingent of Sikhs and fed between 5000 - 10,000 attendees at the Parliament of World's Religions at Salt Lake City, Utah for five full days from October 15 -19, 2015.[23]

EGO AND ITS CONTROL

According to the Sikh faith, ego is considered an obstacle to understanding the truth. By developing humility and providing selfless service, a Sikh hopes to develop a love for all and recognize the presence of Creator/God within. The entire premise and primary goal of being a Sikh is about changing from a self-centered person ("manmukh") to becoming a God-centered person ("gurmukh") in this life.

HUMAN DESIRES AND CONCEPT OF HEAVEN/LIBERATION IN THE SIKH FAITH

According to Sikh beliefs, every human being is divinely blessed with five major desires in order to ensure procreation. These desires are

- the attraction for the opposite gender,
- outrage against injustice,

---

[21] Similar to having separate lunch counters for blacks in America 'til the 1960s.

[22] Selfless service.

[23] http://americansikhcouncil.org/2015/10/28/sikhs-excel-at-the-parliament-o f-worlds-religions/

- the desire for necessary possessions,
- a sense of rational attachments,
- and modest pride of achievements.

All these desires should be exercised in moderation. If these desires get out of control, they then turn into the five major human infirmities or vices:

- Kaam (irresponsible lust),
- Karodh (uncontrollable anger),
- Lobh (unnecessary greed),
- Moh (irrational attachments),
- and Hankaar (arrogant pride).

Unfortunately, most of us have a tendency to become trapped in these vices. Any escape from this eternal penitentiary of vices is recognized as liberation or Heaven in the Sikh faith. The Sikh faith teaches us to strive to achieve liberation during our lives and not after death. It is, in fact, an extremely difficult job. To achieve success, the Sikh faith teaches us to strive for a disciplined life right now.

To emphasize the urgency of achieving and enjoying liberation, the Sikh Gurus have reminded us about the real objective of human life by stating,

> O My Mind! You have received from God your human body,
> This alone is your opportunity to attain unto Him (Godliness).[24]

The Sikh view on the concept of "Heaven, or Liberation," is different from the views in the majority of other faiths.

The major distinction is that most religions consider the concept of "Heaven, or Liberation," to be a part of some unseen afterlife dominion and/or a place "up there somewhere." In contrast, Sikh faith believes heaven or liberation is right here and to be achieved in this life. Heaven and hell in the Sikh faith are a state of mind in the here and now versus an afterlife.

As the Sikh scripture clearly states,

---

[24] SGGS, Page 13

Everyone claims that he/she is going to Heaven out there, but I do not even know, where (such a) heaven is! . . . (Such claimants) not having explored even the mystery of their inner-selves, speak of being able to reach that heaven, just by merely talking. . . . (O my mind,) As long as you hope for going to (such a) heaven; you will not be able to even dwell in the Almighty's Feet. . . . (Understand) Heaven is not some sort of fort (out there) surrounded by a defensive wall, or a township with an embankment around it; I, for one, do not even know about any entrance to such a heaven. . . . Says Kabir, now what more can I say? Except, pronouncing that the real heaven is right here in the company of Saadh Sangat (the Godly-minded persons).[25]

CONCLUSION

The fundamental principles of the Sikh faith align with every humanistic value held by people everywhere of any faith or no faith. Sikh Americans do try to educate others, but only for the sake of removing ignorance in general. Proselytizing is not done as there are no heavenly brownie points earned from conversions.

Once these salient features are understood in the proper context, then the Sikh uniform and turban will automatically fit the paradigm of normality—within the religions familiar to most Americans. The turban and its relevance to the Sikh faith is elaborated in the next chapter.

---

[25] SGGS, Page 1161

THE SIKH TURBAN

HISTORY OF THE TURBAN

What comes to mind when you hear the word "turban"? "Muslim, Sikh, Middle East"? The word "turban" actually, according to the Bible, means a head covering made of cloth wrapped around the head worn by men. If the Bible gives some insight about the turban, then it must be meaningful, right? Now, in the perspective of the Sikh religion, turbans represented a holy figure and royalty. From Guru Nanak's early childhood, he practiced his principles along with keeping his hair uncut and wore a turban. His ideology continued and was passed along to his other nine successors (Gurus 1539–1708).

This is why in the *Guru Granth Sahib*, the religious scripture of the Sikhs, talks about turbans as it is a foundational part of Sikh religion. Guru Granth Sahib Ji, it says, "Having met the Guru, I have put on a tall plumed turban!"[26] There are other references to uncut hair and the turban in the Guru Granth Sahib. "Charming are our uncut Hair, with a Turban on head."[27] "Let living in His presence, with mind rid of impurities be your discipline. Keep the God-given body intact and with a Turban donned on your head."[28]

Throughout Sikh history, the Gurus and many of their followers went through times of pain and suffering to allow the Sikh

---

[26] SGGS (Shri Guru Granth Sahib), Page 74

[27] SGGS, Page 659

[28] SGGS, Page 1084

faith to continue to flourish. Many Muslims, Jains, Buddhists, and Hindus became Sikhs as they found the religion more appealing than their own.[29]

IDENTITY STRUGGLE: CONSEQUENCES OF SIKHS WEARING TURBANS

The visible articles of faith, combined with the turban gifted to the Sikhs, began to "aggravate" prominent Mughal leaders of the early 18th century. The Sikhs encountered the worst period of persecution and the most malicious discrimination against them during the first half of the 18th century by the Mughal kings of South Asia.[30]

Even though the Sikhs passed through very tough ordeals, they survived with honor and established the Sikh rule between 1764–1849.

Later in modern India, Hindu Prime Minister Indira Gandhi,[31] including others (1984–1998), ordered an indiscriminate extermination of the Sikhs with a view to stop them from practicing their faith. In particular, in 1984, the Indian government attacked the holiest house of prayer, the Darbar Sahib in Amritsar. This act led to the killing of over one million Sikhs in the next fifteen years known as the Sustained Sikh Genocide.[32]

SIGNIFICANCE OF THE TURBAN

The turban for Sikhs is much more than the headdress of the Christian Catholic nuns or the hijab of the Muslim women. For the Sikhs, the turban is a religiously mandated article of faith. A "turban material" is a piece of cloth which is made of fine cotton and comes in various sizes/ lengths from 4–7 yards long and a yard in width, typically. The turban

---

[29] The four predominant faiths which were part of the South Asian landscape at that time and still are.

[30] The most prominent leaders were Bahadur Shah (1707–1712), Farrukh Siyar (1712–1719), Mohammad Shah (1719–1748), and Ahmad Shah (1748–1754).

[31] Indira Gandhi (1978–1984), Rajiv Gandhi (1984–1990), Chandra Shekhar (1990–1991) P. V. Narasimha Rao (1991–1996), Atal Bihari Vajpayee (1996–1996) H. D. Deve Gowda (1996–1997), I. K. Gujral (1997–1998).

[32] www.thirdsikhgenocide.org

is also known as Dastaar, Pagg, Paggri, Keski, and Dumala. There are slight variations in their style.

Turbans at various stages of maturity: child to a teenager

Sikh woman in a Keski

The entire process of tying and wearing a turban by a young Sikh American

For young children, a square piece of cotton cloth is used to make a smaller turban, which is called the "patka"! Once a teenager is mature enough to tie and handle a proper turban, then they start to wear a turban regularly. The patka is typically used for sports activities for adults and teenagers. It is easier to handle and will not unravel in more active sports.

A young Sikh American boy wearing a "patka"

The religious significance and also the mandate by Guru Gobind Singh making the turban an article of faith are the reasons Sikhs revere the turban so deeply.

Ever walk out on a cold winter morning and forgot your hat inside? A turban eliminates that problem! Since it is a part of the religious attire, when you step out of that door, not even the icy winds can get to you! As for the color of the turban, as I tell my friends, "if it matches the color of my outfit for the day, it is the turban for the day."

The distinct Sikh identity keeps them on the path of righteousness. When one is so distinguished, there is a personal, ethical and a moral responsibility which has to be taken seriously. This, in turn, keeps the turbaned practicing Sikh on the right path, hopefully.

In other words, Guru Gobind Singh clearly stated, "So long as the Khalsa maintains his 'distinct identity,' He shall remain imbued with my vitality but those who follow the path of the Brahmins (Hindus) I shall no longer give my blessings."[33]

TURBANED SIKHS UNDER BRITISH RULE (1849–1947)

Since the British ruled the Indian subcontinent for over two centuries, they were keenly aware of the Sikhs and their faith. In fact, there were European senior officers serving in the "Khalsa Fauj," Sikh Army of Maharaja Ranjit Singh, the monarch of the Sikh kingdom "Punjab." Those senior European officers, some even holding the rank of general, all had beards and a few wore turbans.

An American, Alexander Houghton Campbell Gardner, a son of Scottish immigrants born in 1785 (in America), actually served in the Sikh Army with rank of a colonel 'til the eve of the Anglo–Sikh war in 1845 with a full beard and turban. So, the British and other Europeans were well aware of the Sikhs and their customs.[34]

---

[33] Sikh Rehatnmanas (proclamations)—the Sikh moral code of conduct

[34] *Warrior Saints: Three Centuries of Sikh Military Tradition* by Amandeep Singh Madra and Parmjit Singh (1999) ISBN:1-86064-490-2 www.ibtauris.com

Colonel Alexander Gardner, an officer in
Maharaja Ranjit Singh's Sikh Army, Punjab, 1834

After the annexation of the Sikh kingdom of Punjab to British India in 1849, the Sikh soldiers of the Sikh kingdom were disarmed and unemployed for quite a number of years. The British slowly reenlisted them into their regiments as they realized the innate potential of these fine soldiers who had faced them on the battlefields not too long ago.

Once the Sikh soldiers became part of the regular British–Indian Armed Forces, they built a mutual respect and trust with the British overlords. The British used the Sikh soldiers for fighting the fiercest of enemies. The Sikh soldiers faced the showers of bullets and shells wearing "turbans" instead of steel helmets or other types of protection.

Sikh valor in battle knows no bounds, as recorded while defending Fort Lockhart in the battle of *"Saragarhi"* in Afghanistan on September 12, 1897. In this famous battle of unprecedented bravery, all twenty-one (21) turbaned Sikh soldiers of the 34th Sikh regiment led by Haveldar Ishar Singh died to a man defending the post against 10,000–14,000 Afghan tribesmen by killing between 600–1,400 of them before giving up their own lives. This episode is one of the eight greatest stories of collective bravery in the 19th and 20th centuries published by UNESCO.[35] All were awarded the highest gallantry awards posthumously.

The 21 turbaned Sikh soldiers at Fort Lockhart
during the Battle of Saragarhi, 1897

During the First World War, while fighting in the battle of Gallipoli (Turkey) June 3–4, 1915, the 14th Sikh Regiment lost 371 brave officers and soldiers. The ends of the enemy's trenches were found blocked with the bodies of Sikh soldiers and of the enemy who died fighting at close quarters. This was the *"chardi kala"* spirit of the "turbaned Khalsa" soldiers.[36]

During the First and Second World Wars, 83,055 turban-wearing Sikh soldiers laid down their lives and 109,045 were wounded when fighting under the command of the Allied Forces.[37]

Sikh soldiers have fought on battlefields across Europe, Asia, Australia, and Africa during the last 150 years and have had a global presence, so how

---

[35] http://defence.pk/threads/battle-of-saragarhi.36709/

[36] Chardi Kala, unbounded ever-uplifting optimism, is part of the Sikh religious–spiritual psyche.

[37] "British Empire, 1914/1920 War," page 237, and "Casualties in the Second World War 1939–45," published in 1951.

can they have gone unnoticed by the powers to be especially in America, because it was the same British and other Europeans whose progeny rule America, today? This seems to be a bad case of acute amnesia!

TURBANED SIKHS IN THE INDIAN MILITARY AND SOCIETAL ATTITUDES

In modern India the Sikh turban is accepted and respected with an unwritten caveat. All Sikh military personnel who are serving in the Indian Armed Forces are authorized to wear turbans, and their uniform includes the turban but not the *"Kirpan."*[38]

However, in June 1984, the Indian Army actually sent out a bulletin in its monthly newsletter, *Baat Cheet*, across the nation, warning and announcing that any and all formally initiated Sikhs must be watched and reported to the authorities immediately. This "declaration" indirectly created an enormous sense of fear throughout Sikh society and the host majority of India. Negative fallout occurred as a result of this. This was tantamount to making a "formal government decree" by branding all religious practicing Sikhs as suspects and terrorists, permanently. This official announcement has not been rescinded in the last 31 years. Due to this one single official announcement, the entire Sikh collective went through over 15 years of slow Indian (Hindu) style extermination of the Sikh populace,[39] with many Sikh officers and soldiers resigning and many others had to cower and shed their physical appearance in order to show their patriotism to the ruling Hindu elite. This was bullying of the entire Sikh population, legally.

Here is what the Indian Army Bulletin had to say:

> Some of our innocent countrymen were administered oath in the name of religion to support extremists and actively participated in the act of terrorism. These people wear a miniature

---

[38] Constitution of India—Defense Services Regulations of 1962, Para 1385, Clause d

[39] www.thirdsikhgenocide.org Over a one million Sikhs murdered by the Indian Regime between 1984–1998.

kirpan round their neck and are called "Amritdharis." Any knowledge of the "Amritdharis" who are dangerous people and pledged to commit murder, arson and acts of terrorism should be immediately brought to the notice of the authorities. These people may appear harmless from outside but they are basically committed to terrorism. In the interest of us all, their identity and whereabouts must always be disclosed. We keep our ears and eyes open; never listen to rumors and malicious propaganda being planned and carried out by the enemy agents.[40]

Notice the language in the statement as it does not contain the word "Sikh," yet it clearly talks about Sikhs. This is literally bullying the Sikhs to death. Their only crime: they were trying to follow and practice their faith.

Since 1978, Sikhs have been harassed and oppressed by the Indian Hindu government through its secret agencies and aided by a myriad of extreme rightwing Hindu organizations. Like other nations, Sikhs in India continue to aspire to have their own independent homeland of Punjab through peaceful means.

TURBANED SIKHS IN THE US

In spite of the historical evidence, in recent years, Sikhs have been subjected to various unpleasant laws relating to the "turban" in the US. Often, the Department of Motor Vehicles in various states will ask a Sikh American to remove their turban in order to take a photograph for their driver's license. A legal threat and sometimes a lawsuit ensues in order for the constitutional right of the citizen to be upheld. It is a nuisance and a constant stumbling block for the regular Sikh American citizen who simply wants to go about his or her business without being subject to legal discriminatory hurdles at every step of the way.

Some states are silent on the turban issue: "Georgia, Kansas, Kentucky, and New Hampshire do not have laws or regulations regarding headgear

---

[40] http://www.sikhcoalition.org/about-sikhs/history/baatcheet-indian-army-bulletin

37

in driver's license photos."[41] In 2010, a father and son were denied the right to take a photograph with their turban for a regular driver's license. The Sikh American organization SALDEF pursued the case and won so that Mr. Singh and his son could acquire their license with an apology: "The DDS apologizes if . . . [the] customer [was] unable to obtain a driver's license or identification card with a photograph of him wearing his dastaar." Additionally, they commented that "The DDS . . . recognizes the rights of Sikhs and members of other faiths to be photographed wearing headgear."[42] Similar examples like this one abound.

CONCLUSION

Sikh Americans have been forced to spend a extraordinary amount of their time and financial resources in establishing that their turban is an integral part of their religious attire and being turbanless is seriously detrimental to their identity. However, the American government does respect the religious and cultural difference and has responded positively to some of the ongoing legitimate demands of the Sikh Americans. Once they are educated about the issues, improvements in accommodation have been made.

But there is still a long way to go to remove the "turban ceiling" in employment, which has been one of the main reasons why thousands of qualified Sikh American men have become self-employed over the last century. The situation is changing, but this subtle bullying must be nipped and better sense must prevail so "everyone" can feel truly equal.

---

[41] http://moritzlaw.osu.edu/electionlaw/litigation/documents/LWVJ.pdf

[42] http://saldef.org/news/georgia-dds/#.VfmXi99Viko

SIKHS IN AMERICA

EARLY HISTORY

The earliest record of Sikhs arriving in America is on April 6, 1899, at Angel Island, San Francisco, California.[43]

It is astonishing that no mention has been made in school textbooks for over 100 years of a highly visible and vibrant religious minority living in the midst of a mostly "Anglo Christian" community, especially in states like California.

In the early part of the 20th century, Sikh settlers came to America in search of jobs and farmland. Between 1899–1915, there were about 7,000 immigrants from Punjab in America, over 85 percent of whom were Sikhs.[44]

Many Sikhs came through Vancouver and then traveled south along the West coast while working in the lumber industry, in railroad construction, and on farms. In California, Sikhs settled in the Sacramento and San Joaquin Valleys because of the land. Some moved further south and settled in the Imperial Valley. Initially, Sikhs worked as farm hands and laborers. Later, they started to lease land and tried their hand at farming as self-employed owners.

The first and oldest Gurdwara which is on the US historical register was established in 1912 in Stockton, California. It was built by these new immigrants.[45] This was the central focus for all organized Sikh religious

---

[43] http://www.sikhpioneers.org/images/Display%20Pictures/005.jpg
San Francisco Chronicle, April 6, 1899.

[44] http://www.pluralism.org/religion/sikhism/america

[45] http://sikhcentury.us/

39

life in America. The Gurdwara was used for traditional occasions, such as birth, marriage, death, as well as political and social activity.

Sikh American men at the Gurdwara, Stockton, CA, 1912

Bullying started from the very beginning for the Sikhs. In this early period, the press often referred to Sikhs as *"Hindoos,"* a patronizing term for Sikhs. Since there were very few Sikhs who had a strong command in the English language, the early settlers never got much of a chance to correct this media-created error.

Sikh immigration to the US was increasing during a period when anti-Chinese/Japanese sentiment was already growing among the European–American settlers in states of California, Oregon, and Washington. Initially, Sikhs were well received by employers in the northwest to work on railroads and in lumber mills. However, white immigrants felt threatened by Sikh immigrants because they would work for low wages. White owners discriminated against Sikh workers by paying them substantially lower wages. White coworkers resented the Sikhs' determined work ethic and being able to work outside the organized labor unions since they were not included as part of the unions.

In Bellingham, Washington, around 1907, 600 white lumber workers attacked the homes of some 250 Sikh millworkers, assaulting them, throwing their possessions out, and herding them to the city jail. One of the articles reported in the Bellingham Herald on September 6, 1907, described the Sikhs as "Hindus . . . dusky aliens . . . turbans of every color of the rainbow."[46]

Bellingham newspapers opposed the violence of the mob but sympathized with the whites to purge the country of Sikhs. Some of the one-sided mob violence engineered by whites was less publicized than incidents that occurred in Seattle and Everett, WA. Real estate brokers in Port Angeles, WA, publicly pledged not to sell property to "Hindoos and Negroes."[47] Sikhs were openly bullied by the people, the system, and the media.

Across the West Coast, the turban-wearing Sikhs were bullied by being commonly referred to as "ragheads."[48] Due to extreme resentment and bias against Asians and Sikhs, new laws were enacted to bar more immigrants from coming from across the Pacific. California passed the Alien Land Act of 1913, which barred "aliens," making them ineligible for citizenship from owning land.

---

[46] http://www.slate.com/blogs/the_vault/2015/02/13/history_of_sikhs_in_america_violence_against_sikh_workers_in_bellingham.html

[47] http://www.pluralism.org/religion/sikhism/america/discrimination

[48] Ibid

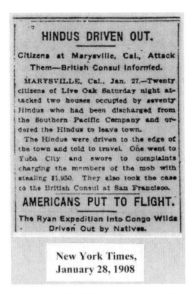

Sikhs (patronizingly called Hindus) bullied by the locals in
Marysville, California, 1908

This first wave of Sikh immigrants garnered enough attention so
that the US Congress passed a racist law in 1917 that was called the
Barred Zone Act, which covered many Asian countries, including British
India, from where immigration would be halted. The act specifically
prohibited the immigrants already settled in America from bringing
their wives. Under these circumstances, it was a very difficult choice
whether to remain or leave, but many of the early Sikhs decided to put
roots down regardless.[49]

More than 85% of all immigrants who came from colonial British India
were all turban-wearing Sikhs. The vast majority were hardy farmers looking
to make a better life, just like immigrants from Europe. The prejudices of
the white society were intense; in spite of that, Sikhs persevered. Many
married Mexican women due to the affinity of food and the fact that there
were other social constraints when marrying whites.

---

[49] http://www.pluralism.org/religion/sikhism/america/discrimination

CHALLENGES TO THE EARLY IMMIGRATION AND CITIZENSHIP LAWS

One of the most famous challenges to the early immigration and citizenship laws was initiated by Bhagat Singh Thind, who came to the US in 1913 to pursue higher education in California, after serving in the British Indian army. Knowing of his military experience he was recruited into the US Army on July 22, 1918, to fight in World War I. He was promoted to acting sergeant and received an honorable discharge on December 16, 1918, with a rating of "excellent." While still serving in the US Army, Thind took the oath for citizenship on December 9, 1918, in uniform from the state of Washington.[50]

Just a few days later, Thind's citizenship was revoked on the grounds that he was not a white man. He immediately applied for citizenship in neighboring Oregon for a second time in 1919. A federal judge heard testimony from both Thind and the Immigration and Naturalization Service (INS) and ruled in Thind's favor by allowing him to become a citizen in early 1920.

The INS appealed to the 9th Circuit Court of Appeals, and the case went to the Supreme Court. In 1923, the Supreme Court ruled in favor of the INS, stating that Thind was not a *"Caucasian"* as commonly understood by the people. This case retroactively denied every Sikh and others from that part of the world by revoking their US citizenship.

Bhagat Singh Thind was not one to give up easily and continued his fight with the government, meanwhile earning a doctorate in theology from the University of California. Finally, in 1935, the 74th Congress passed a law allowing US citizenship for all those veterans who served in World War I, including those from the barred zones, like Dr. Thind. Eventually, after 18 long years, in 1936, Dr. Thind received his US citizenship.

One of the methods used by the Sikhs to fight unjust laws was to fight the system through the courts. Dr. Thind, a great American pioneer, fought bullying by the government against great odds, using all legal means to pave

---

[50] http://www.ccss.org/resources/documents/sikh%20migration%20to%20ca%20_%20 west%20coast.pdf

the way for all Asians immigrants to ultimately to acquire US citizenship. This also paved the way for property ownership by all Asian Americans thereafter.

ADAPTATION AND ASSIMILATION

Since the overwhelming majority of people in power and society at large were European, Christian, and white, the bench mark of "normal" was based on their definition. Anyone who did not fit into that mold was a foreigner, alien, and an outcaste.

For a European, it was very easy to fit into American society. Other than possibly not knowing the commonly spoken English language, "European whites" were invisible and blended right in without creating any kind of waves because the vast majority of the population was white.

In the case of the Sikhs, they had several issues. They were of a different faith, a different shade of color, and the Sikh males wore turbans and beards. Even if the Sikhs spoke impeccable English, it is human nature to be wary of any person or group of people who is different.

Sikhs did adapt very quickly, which included most intermarrying the locals, often of Mexican heritage. On the other hand, assimilation is based on the perception of the host majority. The Sikhs are one of the most adaptable people as they have learnt the local languages and customs of the lands they immigrated to and eventually settled in: Kenya, Tanzania, Uganda, Malaysia, Argentina, New Zealand, Australia, United Kingdom, France, Germany, Italy, Spain, Canada, America, and many other countries. The links with the old homeland eventually decreased, and Sikhs adjusted by assimilating themselves in the new homeland; in this case, America.

The faith of a people, for example, is a personal choice and in no way impinges on anybody else, except that the majority can be prejudiced for a number of reasons beyond the control of the bullied Sikhs.

There are German immigrants known as the Pennsylvania Dutch, including Amish living across America. The Amish have retained their original language and their religious attire, even today. The women have uncut hair covered by bonnets on their head, and men wear long beards and wide brimmed hats, not too different from the Sikhs except that they wear turbans yet have similar uncut beards. America has accepted the Amish as Americans. Sikhs strive for acceptance in America by adapting and adopting the customs of the host culture. However, Sikhs have not been accepted and assimilated in all of American society. Perhaps this double standard is due to the fact that the Amish are white European Christians and the Sikhs are not?

An Amish couple in America

A Sikh couple in America

CHANGE AND GROWTH OF SIKH AMERICANS

Over the years, the numbers and the level of education of Sikhs has changed. Sikh Americans can be categorized into four groups. First were the early immigrants, which included the workers and a small group of students from 1899–1960. My great-grandfather Ram Singh falls in this group as he arrived in Portland, Oregon, in late 1917 as a student. Second were the professionals, such as engineers, doctors, and students, from 1960–1984. The third group were in large part, political and religious refugees from 1984–2010. Finally, the fourth group is primarily the European American Christians and Jewish American converts who adopted the Sikh faith from 1970 onwards.

These groups represent different educational and economic levels during different periods in the last 100-plus years, showing the varying attitudes of the host majority vis-à-vis the Sikhs. Every religious group has a yearning to preserve their heritage and leave a legacy with their progeny, as is the nature of all humans. Sikhs are no different; therefore, they have and still are trying to inculcate the traditional values of their heritage and straddle the wider majority's European Christian based culture. Because of ignorance and bias, the majority many times does not realize that the basic values among the Sikhs and the Christians are actually very similar. Educating everyone about this so that the Sikh American children are less stressed about bullying is the big challenge since the children are put in situations not of their own doing when it comes to religious attire. There are internal challenges as well, and those depend entirely on how important the current generation considers preserving their distinct heritage.

POPULATION OF SIKH AMERICANS

The US Census Bureau does not collect data by religion, thus there is no definitive data on the exact numbers of Sikhs living in the US, although the Pew Research Center has done some work in this respect.[51] Statistics compiled by *Times of India*, an ethnic newspaper out of New York City, used last

---

[51] http://www.pewresearch.org/2012/08/06/ask-the-expert-how-many-us-sikhs/

names to do a census and extrapolate subsets among the (so-called) Indian diaspora. The second most common last name after "Patel" is "Singh." Now, not all Singhs are Sikhs, but all Sikhs are Singhs. The vast majority of Sikhs use family or names of their families or villages as their last names, which reduces the number of Singhs in the census gathering. If all Sikhs did use only "Singh" as their legal last name, then a much larger number would show up in the statistical data. If those names were added to the mix, the numbers would be well over 500,000 Sikhs living in America currently.[52]

In addition to name collection, the Sikhs have used alternate methods to extrapolate populations. The American Sikh Council, while looking at the 200 gurdwaras in the US of which 60 gurdwaras and 8 Sikh institutions are members of the American Sikh Council, a national association of gurdwaras and Sikh institutions across the US,[53] found that there are at least 100,000 adult members in these gurdwara/institutions alone, which translates into at least 300,000 Sikhs, including children. There are many who are not regular and many not even part of any gurdwara. Based on these numbers, the overall population would be over 500,000 across the nation.

STRESSES FACED BY SIKH AMERICAN CHILDREN

Since the Sikh American population is small and spread across the US, it is common to find only one male turbaned child in the entire school. Typically, a male Sikh American child stands out because of the distinguishing religious attire: the turban/patka. Sikh American girls are bullied but at a much lower rate than boys because they are not easily distinguished by the turban. If the school does not teach about the Sikh American heritage, then that misinformation causes ignorance. A climate of ignorance will cause bullies to bully a Sikh American child unless the administration is vigilant in addressing the problem.

---

[52] http://timesofindia.indiatimes.com/world/us/Immigrant-America-and-Patel-tales-US-has-more-than-145000-Patels-and-72642-Singhs/articleshow/19327958.cms

[53] http://www.worldsikhcouncil.org/about/member.html

As a result of ignorance, Sikh American children are left out of certain sports by adult coaches many times because of their turban. The teachers many times refer to the lone Sikh American child as that "Indian kid." Sikh American male children cannot participate in plays as most plays never have a part which can accommodate a turban-wearing child.

There are many challenges and issues, and I will talk more about the stresses faced by Sikh American children in the following chapters.

CHRISTIANITY, JUDAISM, EUROCENTRISM, AND THE BLIND SPOT

"We, the people of this continent, are not fearful of foreigners,
because most of us were once foreigners . . . I say this to you
as the son of immigrants, knowing that so many of you are
also descended from immigrants."[54]

On September 24, 2015, this is what Pope Francis had to say to America in Washington, DC.

WHITE CHRISTIAN MAJORITIES

The definition of who is an "American," in large part, described as "white and Christian." However, this is not the case. For example, I wonder what if a native was asked, "Who is an American?"

I distinctly remember my dad taking my brother and me to a Lenape Indian festival in Westhampton, New Jersey, when I was in 7th grade. All the stalls, exhibits, and most of the people walking around were not white, Hispanic, or black but a group with very unique features, a calm demeanor, smiling, and all wearing a peculiar T-shirt. It took me a bit of thinking to understand what was written on all the T-shirts. It said, "The Original

---

[54] http://www.nytimes.com/2015/09/25/us/pope-francis-congress-speech.html?_r=0

Homeland Security—Defending America since 1469"![55] Here were the real Native Americans who had lived continuously for over 13,000 years were completely sidelined and pretty much forgotten by mainstream "much newer" Americans. The Native Americans were and are acutely aware of who the real Americans are—which is them![56] The rest of us are all, in a way, newcomers, regardless of whether we were born here or somewhere else. Based on personal experience and the experiences of my family members, it is the European Americans who claim to being American; it is pretty much accepted that it is their birthright, while anyone and everyone else has to prove their Americanism or be socially categorized as the interloper/foreigner.

For every Sikh child or adult, it is a given that the following very inoffensive-sounding question will be asked no matter what: "So, where are you from?" Technically, I am a 4th-generation Sikh American since my great-grandfather came to America in late 1917 to study at University of Oregon, Eugene, Oregon; later University of California at Berkley, California; and finally University of Iowa at Ames, Iowa, completing his master's in science. That makes it nearly 100 years, yet the seemingly innocuous question which is invariably loaded is asked of every Sikh, making them feel like outsiders, as though they have just got off the boat and/or are illegal aliens. Most of the time, the question is purposely asked to point out that "you" are a foreigner and have no right to call yourself a "real" American. I was born right here in southern New Jersey. I know several of my close friends who are first generation immigrants from several East European and a few from Western European countries and are rarely asked the same loaded question simply because they are "white" and assumed to be (the "white" definition of) "American." Just as a side note, I am always asked where I am from.

---

[55] When the Christopher Columbus was searching for "India" or the "East Indies," the land of spice and honey, he landed in what is the modern West Indies (Jamaica) in 1469. The same year, the founder of the Sikh faith, Guru Nanak, was born on the other side of the planet in the area Columbus was searching for so desperately.

[56] http://www.indians.org/articles/american-indians.html

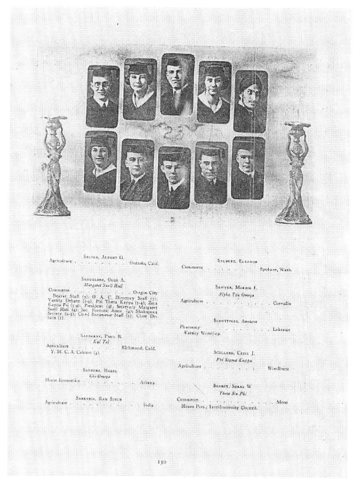

My great grandfather Ram Singh on the top right, University of Oregon, 1921

On March 28, 2015, Roger Moore, the British actor who played the role of James Bond in seven films, made a very similar comment about Idris Elba, another famous black British actor, who was being considered for the role in the upcoming movie, stating, "He is not English-English"![57] Except for Mr. Moore, everyone else can understand the underlying, outright, loaded

---

[57] http://www.nydailynews.com/entertainment/movies/roger-moore-idris-elba-bond-unrealistic-article-1.2165478

bigotry in his statement. The fact is that Idris Elba was born in the United Kingdom, but since he is not "white," therefore, not good enough to play the iconic British role of "James Bond," who has been a white man for all these years. Bigoted humans do play a role in all the daily havoc caused to other humans, and that is bullying.

Bullies bully their victims by interrogative questioning in the following vein, "but you are not American-American," meaning the victim is not "white" and patriotic enough to pass off as an "American"; this is exactly the underlying racism which is played out on a daily basis on adults, and then children use the same methodology against their Sikh American peers.

This mindset and style of questioning can be handled by older teenagers and adults more maturely, but for younger children, it can be very stressful if they are made to feel like outsiders on a daily basis. Many times the fallout is bullying, verbal and/or physical, causing long-term trauma.

This Eurocentrism has been ubiquitous from America, to Canada, to Australia, to New Zealand, to South Africa, to the entire continent of South America, and few more countries, wherever the Europeans landed and took over political power. The European "foreigners" became the "supposed natives" wherever they landed and automatically became American, Australian, Mexican, Brazilian, New Zealander, South African, etc., while all the "real, local, original natives" became second-class citizens and foreigners in their own lands (countries).

ROMANESQUE CONDITIONING

Aside from turbans or headgear of varying types, men across the globe have always sported mustaches and beards. History and part myth has it that Egyptians were the first to introduce a shaven look in men particularly, which was later adopted by the Greeks and Romans through the roving warrior/conqueror Alexander the Great around 330 BC.[58] Shaving their beards and cutting their head hair has been going on in Europe and Asia

---

[58] http://www.todayifoundout.com/index.php/2013/04/the-history-of-shaving/

for a very long time but in a very small minority of elites.[59] In fact, bulk of the populations globally had varying lengths of hair and beards. The Anglo-Saxon tribes on the British Isles were all bearded, unkempt, and pretty rough-looking 'til the Romans brought their shaven style when they invaded them. Until World War I, many European men had long hair and were asked to cut them in order to join the armed forces. Yet many of the European armed forces allowed their officers in many wings to have short beards. Going back in time, slaves and men who were defeated during a war were punished and had to shave their heads and faces, which has been going on for many millennia, from Europe to the Far East.

The Chinese men all had long hair in plaits and beards until the early part of the last century and were only cut when penalized for a crime.[60] Due to internal political changes[61] and the advent of the European influence through Christian missionary activity, the opium trade, general interaction with westerners, and finally with the advent of communism, the shaving and cutting of their naturally long hair came to a rapid decline.

From times past, modern man's removal of facial hair and shearing their locks off their heads is a recent phenomenon with a very short span on the long timeline of history and not something that has eons of history. The only men shaving their heads and faces were those that were indentured slaves or punished by kings and governments.

Most written material—namely, old historical textbooks and various religious literatures—all contains plenty of positive references to long head hair and full beards. But it is eerie that the articles and blogs by Europeanized writers on the modern-day Internet referencing the same hair and beards try to downplay the role and importance of the same. This is all thanks to modernity, what I call the "Romanesque conditioning"; hence, many ignore the reality of the recent past and want to rewrite the "hairy historical truth" to suit their new comfort zone.

---

59 http://www.moderngent.com/history_of_shaving/history_of_shaving.php

60 http://en.wikipedia.org/wiki/Long_hair

61 Communism

Surveys are sometimes designed to get a desired result. A recent survey about what kind of men British women like done by the British newspaper *The Mail* showed that women overwhelmingly liked clean-shaven men.[62] Little do we realize that the entire survey is of white women from a particular country with a distinct Western culture, therefore, the desired results. Surveys and results depend on many variables, not to mention religion, cultural norms, country, economic situation, race, color, country, etc.

People love taking their own pictures and then putting it on social media. Adding to their vanity is the media's general advertising, which invariably show hairless white men and women by and large. Sometimes it becomes hard to distinguish whether the person is a man or woman as shaving of men seems to have feminized them and many times transposed them into looking like women, especially when shaven men have long hair. If men were supposed to look like women, they would never have had beards and mustaches naturally. Societies go through change, but typically it is a "herd mentality" and what is popular or trending becomes the norm, hence, normal.

Sikh Americans are in the minority when it comes to issues such as facial hair and turbans, and it becomes abnormal since the majority rules a trend, regardless of the effect, and will always justify their own premise for the silliest of reasons. But it does not give the majority the right to vilify the minority for no other reason other than their own discomfort since it reminds many that they are cutting/shaving their own facial hair and, more importantly, they are going against their own religious traditions. Further, their own religious prophets had full beards and proper turbans whom they revere. A conundrum indeed!

---

[62] http://www.dailymail.co.uk/femail/article-2110758/As-study-reveals-women-prefer-men-clean-shaven-lifelong-beard-hater-KATHRYN-KNIGHT-asks-stars--Sexier-whisker.html

DETURBANIZING THEIR OWN

History holds witness that Jesus Christ, the divine teacher of all Christians,[63] had long hair and sported a beard. Churches around the globe have millions of depictions of Jesus, and none have long hair or beard missing, but the obvious turban is missing. Every story told, including the pictures depicting Jesus in any kind of a book, be it a children's comic or a theological treatise, all the holy men who came to Bethlehem at his birth, including Joseph, his earthly father, all had long hair, beards, and wore turbans. In fact, everyone during that period in history and in that region of the Mid-East had the very same attire. However, Jesus did not wear a turban according to modern-day Christian history.[64] We have to remember that history, especially religious history, can fall to whims of the personal biases and whims of the writer; therefore, historical truth can be elusive.

In early 2015, I wrote letter to the United States Conference of Catholic Bishops in Washington, DC, the policy arm of the Roman Catholic Church, in order inquire about the role of the turban as it pertains to Jesus. I was fortunate to get a response back from the Secretariat of Catholic Education. My inference from the reply I received clearly indicates that Jesus Christ did, in fact, wear a turban.

---

[63] At last count there were over 250 sects/denominations of Christianity across the US.

[64] Refer to the letter from the United States Conference of Catholic Bishops, March 25, 2015

Karanveer Pannu   February 27, 2015

3 Evergreen Dr

Voorhees, NJ 08043

United States Conference of Catholic Bishops

3211 Fourth Street, NE

Washington, DC 20017

Ref: Did the historical Jesus Christ ever wear a 'turban'?

Dear Sir,

I am studying comparative religion in my high school. I have some unanswered questions and I cannot think of a better source than your esteemed office to respond to my query.

From my research I have concluded that when Jesus Christ was born (2,015 years ago), everyone in the Middle East was of Arab decent or Arab looking (for a lack of a better example – Palestinian looking), therefore if all the holy men of that time (also the ones who came at the birth of Christ) which includes 'Mary's husband 'Joseph' wore turbans. In fact literally everybody and especially religious men always wore turbans as reference to turbans is clearly stated in the Old Testament and the New Testament.

1. So the first question I have, did Jesus Christ being a divine teacher wear a turban?
2. Secondly, if everyone around him wore a turban, why did he not wear a turban?
3. Third, what historic evidence is available to prove that he never wore/ tied a turban?
4. Since the modern day Christian Bible or the New Testament was written approximately four centuries after the passing away of Jesus what evidence is there to support about his precise ethnicity?

I would appreciate if you could provide me with meaningful answers and material related to my questions. My apologies in advance in case I have erred in the manner I have asked my questions as my intent is only to learn and nothing else.

Thanking you in advance for your consideration and looking forward to hearing from you.

Respectfully,

Karanveer Pannu
11th Grade Student

Secretariat of Catholic Education
3211 Fourth Street, NE • Washington DC 20017 • 202-541-3132•202-541-3390

Karanveer Pannu
3 Evergreen Drive
Voorhees, NJ 08043

March 25, 2015

Dear Karanveer,

Thank you for the letter of February 27, 2015 asking about particular aspects of the life of Jesus.

I believe the New Testament can be of assistance in answering your questions about Jesus. In the Infancy narratives there is reference to Jesus being from Nazareth. This speaks of his origins within the Jewish community. Also, I suggest a historical reference in Works of *Josephus* who wrote a history at the time of Jesus, and in which Jesus is also referenced.

The New Testament does not point out anything about Jesus that would have set him apart from his peers. He is not seen as different in any way. In fact, the villagers scorned him as a commoner by referencing his being the "Son of Joseph and Mary".

So, Karanveer, I believe Jesus did and acted as was common for his time. I think he would have worn what was expected of him, prayed as was expected of him, and lived as was expected of him. I also believe that is what makes his Incarnation as the Second Person of the Blessed Trinity so beautiful.

I hope that this is of assistance to you. Good luck with your studies and schooling.

God bless you,

Sister John Mary, O.P.
United States Conference of Catholic Bishops

According to the letter (above), it is pretty clear that Jesus Christ did wear a turban!

If Jesus Christ did wear a turban, then it is strange that he is not depicted wearing one anywhere in Europe, Australia, South America, or North America—for that matter, any locale where there has been European influence. Furthermore, why do none of "his" two billion followers wear a turban either? If Jesus is considered literally the "son of God" and all "his" followers want to be Jesus-like, then why do they not dress like him? Logic states that if all the followers did indeed emulate Jesus, i.e., spiritually and physically, wouldn't it please "him" immensely?

Modern Eurocentric (Christian) theological writers, academics, historians, sociologists, and others have done away with long hair, shaving their beards and not wearing a turban when their own divine leader did so. So, it is uncannily strange that over two billon Christians do not resemble their own spiritual leader, who, in fact, had long hair, sported a beard, and wore a turban. In fact, only a small portion of the clergy of the larger Christendom, like the Greek Orthodox, the Armenian Orthodox, the Russian Orthodox, the Syrian Orthodox, the Serbian Orthodox, the Croatian Orthodox, the Eastern Orthodox, to name a few, sport beards with "head coverings" but still no turban. Most, if not all, clergymen are shaven, including the pope. The real question is if any Christian loves their "heavenly father" and, especially, his beloved "son" so much, shouldn't they emulate him from the external/physical attornments along with all the other righteous spiritual attributes? Another blind spot!

In the photograph (below), the Sikh soldiers are bearded, turbaned, and in uniform following their religious obligation and lawful occupation, saddling both in a fine manner. I mentioned beards and head coverings for the Christian priests earlier, and the photograph below clearly shows an archbishop sporting a full beard with a veiled hat covering his head in 1945. The British officer next him is shaven and in uniform, though he is more than likely a Christian.

Archbishop Damaskinos of Greece, ashore at Salonika in a visit to the 1914–1918 War Cemetery, March 1 1945. The purpose of the visit was to bless the monument to the troops who fell in action there. Here he is seen meeting men of the 4th Indian Division. This image exemplifies a unique aspect of Sikhism. The Sikh soldiers are wearing both their military and religious uniform in interesting contrast to the other figures in the image, who are either military or religious in their dress and role.

The three soldiers on the right are of the Sikh faith
meeting the Archbishop Damaskinos

Christian nuns are another highly visible example of women covering themselves completely, from head to toe—no different than a modern-day Muslim woman with a hijab. My parents, grandparents, and great-grandparents all attended Catholic schools from the 1900s to the early 1980s, and every one of those schools were run by "habit-wearing" nuns who looked no different than a Muslim woman in their very normal attire.[65] All these nuns were mostly European white women and very foreign-looking based on my heritage. I have often wondered why many of my peers are curious about what's underneath my turban, but the same question never comes up when Sikhs have interacted with habit-wearing nuns. My turban is checked and scanned every time I enter any government building and especially at the airport by the security personnel. However, I have personally never observed the same procedure being done to nuns.

A stone's throw from where I live, there is a nunnery, or a convent, called "The Little Servant Sisters of the Immaculate Conception" (TLSSTIC), which has nuns with their heads covered, except now their foreheads have started to show and their skirts have started to get a bit shorter, revealing their ankles and more.[66] Catholic nuns all over the globe, even in 2015, still mostly cover their hair with a habit. To the lay person, especially any non-European, their attire is very different. Furthermore, within the vast Catholic Church, nuns wear all kinds of styles of head coverings, many which are much more unusual looking than even the mundane Muslim hijab. Once European Americans ponder on this, then understanding the Sikh American turban becomes a nonissue.

In an recent study done on November 26, 2014, aptly called "Stereotyping is alive and well when it comes to Muslim and Sikh religious symbols in Canada: poll," the mostly white citizens who were polled stated, "Nearly 90 per cent of Canadians have no problem with a nun wearing her habit in public and 80 per cent support the wearing of a kippa (a Jewish cap) in public." Yet when it came to Muslims and Sikhs, the same folks had opposing views, making them deeply hypocritical.[67] This is troubling since

---

[65] A full hijab and robes till the ankles.

[66] http://www.blessededmundcenter.com/little_servant_sisters.php Cherry Hill, NJ

[67] http://www.theprovince.com/life/Stereotyping+alive+well+when+comes+Muslim+Sikh+religious+symbols+Canada+poll/10413196/story.html

these biases do have a trickle-down effect onto their own children, who then carry on the bullying cycle of Sikh children or others like them.

Catholic nuns, over 705,000[68] of them, do look different and distinguished in over 150 countries[69] they exist, yet it is rare for the host populations to question or mock their external–physical attire. Again, why are Sikhs questioned for wearing their religious attire for reasons analogous to the Christian Catholic nuns in some way is strange and very perplexing.

It will be extremely interesting to observe if ever "nuns" decided to work in corporate America while keeping their "normal attire" intact! I wonder if they be allowed to keep their head coverings or would they be forced to remove them? Most of corporate America is still by and large European American and Christian, but they have never had to confront the issue I am bringing up.

Like I mentioned earlier, I took it upon myself to do research and formulated a set of questions inquiring into the history and reasons for beards and turbans in the Abrahamic traditions. The extremely vague answers to my specific questions in reference to the attire of Jesus Christ and what are the actual reasons for nuns to wear their traditional religious garb were very revealing. It is interesting to note that on the letter head of the response by the nuns there is a painting of Jesus with his disciples—Jesus has long hair and is bearded like the others, while some of his disciples are turbaned, and yet the completely head- and body-covered nuns of the TLSSTIC are tongue-tied when it came to answering my questions, especially when it came to Jesus Christ.

---

[68] http://cara.georgetown.edu/caraservices/requestedchurchstats.html based on 2014 statistical data

[69] http://www.catholic-hierarchy.org/country/sc1.html based on November 2005 statistical data

Little Servant Sisters of the Immaculate Conception   April 6, 2015
1000 Cropwell Rd
Cherry Hill, NJ 08003

Ref: Why do Nuns wear a habit and cover their head?

Dear Madam,

I am studying comparative religion in my high school. I have some unanswered questions and I cannot think of a better source than your esteemed office to respond to my query.

1. Please enlighten me as to why Catholic Nuns cover their head with the customary 'habit' in particular?
2. Do Nuns cut their hair and/or allowed to do so by the Church authorities?
3. Are the clothes worn by all Nuns customary to be full length (head to ankles)?
4. Why have some Nuns stopped wearing the 'habit', even though they are practicing Nuns?
5. Does that not mean that they have fallen from 'grace'?
6. Did Jesus Christ being a divine teacher and/or a 'son of god' wear a turban?
7. Secondly, if everyone around him wore a turban, why did he not wear a turban?
8. Third, what historic evidence is available to prove that he never wore/tied a turban?
9. Since the modern day Christian Bible or the New Testament was written approximately four centuries after the passing away of Jesus what evidence is there to support his precise ethnicity?

I would appreciate if you could provide me with meaningful answers and material related to my questions. My apologies in advance in case I have erred in the manner I have asked my questions as my intent is only to learn and nothing else.

Thanking you in advance for your consideration and looking forward to hearing from you.

Respectfully,
Karanveer Singh Pannu
11th Grade Student

LITTLE SERVANT SISTERS OF THE IMMACULATE CONCEPTION,

1000 CROPWELL ROAD, CHERRY HILL, NJ 08003

April 14, 2015

Karanveer Pannu
3 Evergreen Drive
Voorhees, NJ 08043

Dear Karanveer:

We wish you all the best in your study of comparative religion, including the history of Middle Eastern religions, Judaism, Christianity and Islam.

In turn, we offer you our Paschaltide greetings in our celebration of the Risen Christ and beautiful Easter traditions.

Yes, the Passion of Christ has been transformed into its opposite – His Glory. The promise of the Resurrection in Jesus Christ is the axiom that shapes our whole temporal and eternal life. This is precisely the cause of our deep joy and hope.

God's blessings to you in your academic life and charitable activities!

Yours sincerely,

Little Servant Sisters

Little Servant Sisters

I am confused by the hypocrisy of our society. If a black or white Christian woman becomes a "nun," she is considered devout and devoted to her "god," but why is a Muslim woman who is also devout and devoted to her "god" considered oppressed and/or a fundamentalist? This is indeed an enigma which society chooses to ignore—a blind spot!

Furthermore, a person of the Sikh faith who is doing the exact same thing, which is being devout and devoted to the fundamental postulates of their faith's teachings, get covertly and overtly ostracized by society for looking or being different. On the other hand, if a nun is walking down Main Street, probably no one will taunt, insult, or bully her for her "hijab-like head covering" and overall flowing religious garb, yet a turbaned Sikh American can rarely walk down Main Street before someone driving by will yell a slur, honk their horn, or flip their middle finger and get bullied, as this is an experience every Sikh American goes through on an regular basis across America, including me. Hundreds of thousands of Sikhs in America can relate to this issue for the last 100-plus years. The bigger question is why the double standard by the European Americans who are overwhelmingly Christian and who all supposedly came to America for religious freedom?[70]

I call this a "Eurocentric blind spot"! While driving, we all know there is a blind spot when looking in the rearview and/or side mirrors, but many choose to ignore at their own peril. Just like while driving on a highway with hundreds of other cars, some humans choose to ignore other cars at their peril and then curse when they suddenly realize that there is a car right next to them, making them uncomfortable. Similarly, the majority in our country have this "blind spot" and either do not realize it or choose to ignore it, probably because it is simply more comfortable to hold onto the status quo rather than accept the fact that Sikh Americans are as American as apple pie. I wonder if Sikh American turbans and Muslim American hijabs remind the Christian majority in America who happen to be of mostly

---

[70] Even though most belong to the over 250 sects/denominations of "general Christianity."

European descent of their own inadequacies of not being able to follow the edicts of their own faith properly.

The two photographs below, one is of a habit-wearing Catholic nun on the left and the other is a turban-wearing retired Sikh soldier. The point of the two photographs is for the reader to ponder on both the head coverings. The strangeness of either of the head coverings just depends on the perspective of the reader. Yet at the same time, if the viewer is educated about both faiths, then both head coverings are equally normal.

A nun from the St. Mary Catholic Convent, USA

A retired Sikh British officer in London, UK

The Old Testament of the Jewish faith has very clear instructions about religious headgear. We read in Exodus, "For Aaron's sons you shall make tunics, and you shall make sashes for them, and you shall make 'headpieces or turbans' for them, for glory and beauty" (Exodus 28:40). They were also to wear "linen trousers" (verse 42) reaching from the waist to the thighs. This clothing was to be worn "when they come into the tabernacle of meeting, or when they come near the altar to minister in the holy place" (verse 43). Priests wore a "turban" (Exodus 28:4, 40) while officiating at the temple. This is confirmed by both the literature and archaeological remains of the period.[71]

Abraham the Jewish Patriarch with a full beard and a complete turban.

Turbans have been worn by ordinary Jews for a very long time, but as time passed, as many things religious humans do, i.e., found an easier way and did away with this important article of faith, probably because they found it too cumbersome. In the Middle East, even today, turbans and head coverings are common, even though Eurocentric modernity is bringing change fast. Most Jews always wore turbans as they also had

---

[71] http://www.cogwriter.com/triumph.htm

long hair.[72] For example, the patriarch of Judaism is Abraham, who has traditionally been depicted as bearded and turban-wearing.[73]

In the effort to better understand the role of the turban in Judaism, I sent a letter to several national Jewish organizations asking why modern Jews do not wear turbans.

---

[72] http://www.bible-history.com/links.php?cat=39&sub=463&cat_name=Manners+%26+-Customs&subcat_name=Clothing Headdress, Turbans, and Hair (HEADDRESS) The Jews of Bible times gave much attention to the care of their hair. The young people loved to wear it long and curled (Song of Solomon 5:11), and they were proud to have thick and abundant hair (II Samuel 14:25,26). Middle-aged men and priests would occasionally cut their hair but very little. Baldness was scarce and suspicion of leprosy was often attached to it. Thus when the youth said of Elisha, "Go up, thou bald head" (II Kings 2:23), it was using an extreme curse, for the prophet being a young man, may not actually have been bald-headed. Men would not cut their beards, but allow them to grow long (II Samuel 10:4,5). Beards would be anointed with oil often. In public the Jews always wore a turban, for at certain seasons of the year it is dangerous in Israel to expose the head to the rays of the sun. This turban was of thick material and passed several times around the head. It was somewhat like our handkerchief and was made of linen, or recently of cotton. The patriarch Job and the prophet Isaiah mention the use of the turban as a headdress (Job 29:14; Isaiah 3:23). In place of the turban, the Palestinian Arabs today for the most part, wear a head veil called "Kaffieh" which hangs down over part of their garment. *** The Bible teaches that it is a shame for a man to have long hair, and is a sign of rebellion against authority, according to 1 Corinthians 11. Absalom clearly was a rebel. Even in the OT, men (especially the priests, the examples to the rest of Israel) cut their hair short - see Ezekiel 44:20. [Manners And Customs of Bible Lands]

[73] http://people.ucalgary.ca/~elsegal/Shokel/900406_Turbans.html

Karanveer Pannu   April 9, 2015
3 Evergreen Dr
Voorhees, NJ 08043

Head Rabbi – Dean
Beth Medrash Govoha
617 6ᵗʰ St
Lakewood, NJ 08701

Ref: Why do modern Jews not wear turbans?

Dear Sir/Rabbi,

I am studying comparative religion in my high school. I have some unanswered questions and I cannot think of a better source than your esteemed office to respond to my query. There is so much information some possibly accurate and some not, on the internet, therefore I wanted your office to please respond so I get the right answers.

1. If Abraham the founder of Judaism wore a turban, had long hair and a beard, then why do most Jews not adhere to and/or being selective in following the revered founder of the Faith?

2. If traditionally Jews wore turbans why have most of them done away with them, in the last 1-3 centuries and now wear hats, etc?

3. What is the religious role of turbans, head coverings, yarmulkes, kippas in the Jewish Faith?

4. What is the religious significance of (hair) beards and mustaches in the Jewish faith?

5. Since the Old Testament –Jewish Bible does contain clear references to religious injunctions of the 'linen turban' and 'long undergarments' then why these in particular are not followed at all, yet other physically less challenging traditions of food rules, etc, have been followed more strictly?

I would appreciate if you could provide me with meaningful answers and material related to my questions. My apologies in advance in case I have erred in the manner I have asked my questions as my intent is only to learn and nothing else.

Thanking you in advance for your consideration and looking forward to hearing from you.

Respectfully,

Karanveer Pannu
11th Grade Student

בית מדרשו של רבנו הגאון רבי אהרן קוטלר זצוק״ל

BETH MEDRASH GOVOHA

L   A   K   E   W   O   O   D

Karanveer Pannu

3 Evergreen Dr.

Voorhees, NJ 08043

April 28, 2015

Dear Karanveer,

Thank you so much for your letter dated April 9, 2015 and for reaching out to us. We wish you much luck in your studies and are hopeful you will succeed.

In response to your questions, we do not have any idea what type of garments our forefathers wore. Garments were worn out of respect.

A head covering worn by men is done as a symbol of fear of G-d; a constant reminder that G-d is always present.

There are no religious implications in linen turbans and long undergarments.

I do hope we have been able to be of assistance to you.

Once again, best of luck in your studies.

Sincerely,

Rabbi Moshe Levin

I received only one reply from the Beth Medrash Govoha, an ultra-orthodox rabbinical college in Lakewood, New Jersey. Their reply was vague.[74] If there are no religious implications for wearing the turbans by Jewish men, why would they wear them for thousands of years 'til the recent past?

I also sent a similar letter to a few Islamic national organizations within the United States. Most did not reply, with the exception of two organizations. The Council on American–Islamic Relations (CAIR) did reply with a hand-written acknowledgment card, and I appreciated it. However, they did not want to answer any of my written questions and wanted me to call them for better clarity.

The second response was from the Islamic Society of North America (ISNA), which was probably the clearest answer to my questions by far. ISNA answered all the questions. They were explicit in defining their responses because there were so many categories in Islam, it can be difficult for the lay person to make it a little more black and white. Based on ISNA's letter, in regards to turbans, "So for wearing the turban, Muslim scholars are in agreement that wearing the turban or headgear for men is considered recommended . . . that God and his Prophet have not explicitly commanded it to be done but rather recommended . . . there are traditions of the Prophet Muhammad that describe him wearing a piece of headgear and a turban but there are none that require Muslim men to wear it." It is clear that that the turban has been traditionally worn but not commanded as an article of faith.

The women's head coverings are handled in the following manner: "For women however, the headscarf is considered obligatory. This is not so much in terms of belief or doctrine but rather on the rules of modesty for both genders." Since it is not part of the belief or doctrine, it is not an article of faith either.

---

[74] 6,600 students studying religion exclusively at the undergraduate and graduate level

Karanveer Pannu   April 8, 2015
3 Evergreen Dr
Voorhees, NJ 08043

Islamic Society of North America (ISNA)
P.O. Box 38
Plainfield, IN 46168

Ref: Why do Muslims not wear turbans?

Dear Sir,

I am studying comparative religion in my high school. I have some unanswered questions and I cannot think of a better source than your esteemed office to respond to my query. There is so much information some possibly accurate and some not, (on the internet and in books), therefore I wanted your office to please respond so I get the right answers.

1. If Mohammad the founder of Islam wore a turban, had long hair and a beard, then why do most Muslims not adhere to and/or being selective in following the revered founder of the Faith?
2. If traditionally Muslims wore turbans why have most of them done away with them in the last 1-2 centuries, since most other traditional rules of food and prayer are still followed strictly?
3. What is the role of turbans, head coverings, in the Muslim Faith?
4. What is the religious significance of (hair) beards and shaving mustaches in the Muslim Faith?
5. What is the reason for the niqab, hijab and other religious coverings for especially women and is there clear reference to it in the holy Quran?

I would appreciate if you could provide me with meaningful answers and material related to my questions. My apologies in advance in case I have erred in the manner I have asked my questions as my intent is only to learn and nothing else.

Thanking you in advance for your consideration and looking forward to hearing from you.

Respectfully,

Karanveer Pannu
11th Grade Student

The Islamic Society of North America

Islamic Society of North America
P.O. Box 38
Plainfield, IN 46168

April 21, 2015

Mr. Karanveer Pannu
3 Evergreen Drive
Voorhees, NJ 08043

RE: Your letter correspondence on "Why Muslims do not wear turbans?"

Dear Mr. Pannu,

Thank you for contacting the Islamic Society of North America. Before we begin, there are some preliminary issues we need to understand first. In Islamic practice and law, actions are divided into five categories: obligatory, recommended, permissible, disliked and unlawful.

Now to answer your questions:

Your first question is in regards to the Prophet (peace and blessings of God be upon him) wearing the turban, had long hair, and a beard. You also mentioned who most Muslims do not adhere or being selective in following. Going back to our preliminary sentence, actions are divided into the five categories. So for wearing the turban, Muslim scholars are in agreement that wearing the turban or headgear for men is considered recommended. What we mean be recommended is that God and his Prophet have not explicitly commanded it to be done but rather recommended. If one abstains from doing what is recommended it is not a sin, but if one does what is recommended one is rewarded. So there are traditions of the Prophet Muhammad that describe him wearing a piece of headgear and a turban but there are none that require Muslim men to wear it. We do see several scholars, imams and even lay Muslims wearing the turban or at least a kufi (A hat that Muslim men typically wear that vary in style).

As far as the hair, to grow or have the hairstyle of the Prophet Muhammad (peace and blessings of God be upon him) out of love and to emulate him is a recommended act but not obligatory.

For the beard, the majority of scholars hold that it is unlawful to shave off the beard if one can grow one. The minority position is it is offensive to shave the beard off. This is due to several traditions of the Prophet (peace and blessings be upon him that explicitly command male believers to grow the beard. The majority also hold that the recommended beard to be at least fist-length. They differ on whether one can trim the beard and also what in the face constitutes a beard. For example, one position holds that what they mean by beard is the hair that grows on the chin area.

Now with any religious tradition, you will have a wide spectrum of its adherents and their frequency of practice. At one end you will have nominal Muslims who are Muslim in name only and rarely following the practices taught in the religion. You will also find Muslims who try to practice all aspects of the religion. This is human nature.

For your second question you asked about turbans and doing away with them as opposed to food and prayer. Again this goes with how they are categorized on that five value scale. We have already discussed the rulings on the turban, so we will not replicate it again here. As far as the five daily prayers and diet restrictions, these are

Headquarters: P.O.Box 38(mail) . 6555 South County Road 750 East (express mail and packages) . Plainfield . Indiana 46168
(317) 839-8157 . info@isna.net . www.isna.net

ISNA's Office for Interfaith and Community Alliances : 110 Maryland Avenue NE . Suite 304 . Washington DC 20002
(202) 544-5656

The Islamic Society of North America

considered obligatory. Obligatory in a sense that God or his Prophet have explicitly commanded that it be followed. Now why the change in headgear in the last two centuries? This is more of a cultural historical discussion than religious.

Your third question has been already been answered in question #1. For women however, the headscarf is considered obligatory. This is not so much in terms of belief or doctrine but rather on the rules of modesty for both genders. For men, they must cover between the navel and knees. Anything between those areas are considered nakedness and cannot be shown in public and or in front of non-related people. For women, they must cover all but face and hands and some include feet. This is also in terms of public and or in front of non-related people.

The fourth question deals with the religious significance of the beard and shaving the mustache. Part of it was answered earlier in terms of the practice of the Prophet Muhammad (peace and blessings of God be upon him) and his explicit command to do so, but he also said to trim the mustache. Trimming meaning so one can see the pink of one's upper lip. This was also to distinguish oneself from other religious traditions who did not trim the mustache.

Your final question was partially dealt with in our answer to question #3. Niqab refers to a headcovering that leaves the eyes exposed. This position in covering is considered a minority position whereas the majority of scholars have held that the face may be shown.

As far as the textual evidence, we must first talk about the core sources of Islam in relation to proofs to which law, ethics and practice may be derived from. In Sunni Islam, there are four agreed upon sources. The first is the Quran, where Muslims believe it to be the Word of God. The second source is called the Sunnah, which is anything the Prophet Muhammad said, did or approved of. The third source is called Ijma or unanimous consensus of the scholars. The final source is called Qiyas or analogy.

So in terms of textual evidence, there are two Quranic verses for the hijab. The first is in Surah 24:31 and the second is Surah 33:59. There is also Hadith (a written record of the sayings and or actions of the Prophet) evidence. *"Aisha reported that Asma' the daughter of Abu Bakr came to the Messenger of Allah while wearing thin clothing. He approached her and said: 'O Asma'! When a girl reaches the menstrual age, it is not proper that anything should remain exposed except this and this. He pointed to the face and hands."* [Abu Dawud]. Finally, there is unanimous consensus from the scholars that hijab is obligatory. They disagree to the extent of what is covered and contexts.

We hope that our answers to your questions will suffice. If you need further clarification, feel free to email me at ehopida@isna.net.

Sincerely,

Edgar Hopida
Communications Director
Islamic Society of North America

Headquarters: P.O.Box 38 (mail) . 6555 South County Road 750 East (express mail and packages) . Plainfield . Indiana 46168
(317) 839-8157 . info@isna.net . www.isna.net

ISNA's Office for Interfaith and Community Alliances : 110 Maryland Avenue NE . Suite 304 . Washington DC 20002
(202) 544-5656

On the other hand, Sikhs are commanded to have "uncut hair covered by a turban," which is an article of faith. Formally initiated Sikhs who have taken *"Khande De Phaul"* (formal initiation ceremony), wear "long cotton breeches" akin to the "linen trousers" mentioned earlier. So, it very clear that Sikhs are doing their best to follow the dictates of their faith out of love for their faith and not fear; whereas, in my opinion, Christians and, especially, the Jews have done away and/or do not care to follow the religious dictates of their faith. The only exceptions to religiously mandated breeches among Christians are the Mormons sect/denomination and, among the Jews, the Hasidic sect/denomination.[75]

Breeches of the Hasidic-Jews

---

[75] http://bookofmormononline.net/#/commentary/1135604101 He shall put on the holy linen coat, and he shall have the linen breeches upon his flesh, and shall be girded with a linen girdle, and with the linen mitre shall he be attired: these are holy garments; therefore shall he wash his flesh in water, and so put them on.

Breeches of the Sikhs

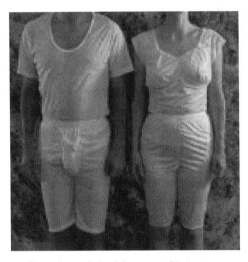

Breeches of the Mormon-Christians

SERVING OUR COUNTRY

Sikh Americans are not simply patriotic like anyone else but are truly vested in the ideals of freedom, liberty, and justice for all as those are the very core values of the Sikh faith. In order to uphold those values, it is an automatic reaction for all able-bodied men and women to be able to serve their country with pride. But unfortunately, the greatest country on Earth, which I call home, disallows me to serve freely due to my uncut hair/beard and the mandatory turban, which to me is upholding the highly cherished values in our (US) constitution.

The first Sikh American to serve America proudly with his religious uniform intact was Dr. Bhagat Singh Thind, who joined the US Army in July 1918 and was honorably discharged as a sergeant at the end of World War I.[76] Later, many turbaned Sikhs served in the US Armed Forces until the tenure of President Ronald Reagan. President Reagan was instrumental in changing the rule within the military which stated that from here on, no one could serve unless they were completely shaven with no religious head gear. In and around 1982, this new rule went into effect, stopping all new turban-wearing Sikh Americans recruits from entering and serving in the military permanently. The photographs below are of career officers who entered and served before 1982 with exemplary service to their country—the United States of America.

Colonel Arjinderpal Singh Sekhon

---

[76] He later earned a doctorate in theology from the University of California, Berkley, CA.

Colonel Gopal Singh Khalsa

Colonel GB Singh

Sergeant Sevak Singh Kroesen

Sergeant Kirbir Singh Grewal

Major Parbhur Singh Brar

From around 1982–2009, no turbaned Sikh American could join the US Armed Forces. In October 2009, after a 27-year gap, Dr. Kamaljit Singh Kalsi joined the US Medical Core but not before jumping through many legal hurdles. Many senior representatives, including my father from the American Sikh Council, formerly known as World Sikh Council - America Region, held several closed door meetings with the army brass at the Pentagon for over a year, which finally paved the way for cracking the door open and eventually allowing the Sikhs to serve proudly—though with a caveat.[77] Even today, an exemption is required

---

[77] http://www.worldsikhcouncil.org/press/2014/24Jan2014.html

for a "bearded–turbaned Sikh" from the company commander, without which one still cannot serve.

Current quirky rules only allow those Sikhs to serve who have special skills which the US Armed Forces need. This creates plenty of wiggle room to discriminate and/or be selective. Only three turbaned Sikh men are currently serving in the US Army. Major Kalsi holds an MD and was an ER physician; Captain Rattan holds a BS in engineering, an MBA, and a DMD in dentistry; and the third soldier, Corporal Lamba, holds a MS in structural engineering but was allowed in for his language skills. In other words, if these three men, who are over-qualified for their positions, did not have these extra qualifications, they would be much less likely to be given a chance to serve. These unbalanced rules fly in the face of the basic articles of our constitution. Not a single Sikh has been allowed so far to join any of the three academies—namely the naval, army or the air force academy—as a cadet to become an officer and serve like anyone else.

A young Iknoor Singh, currently a sophomore at Hoftra University in Long Island, NY, filed suit in court against the ROTC and recently won a victory on June 12, 2015, to be able to join without giving up his religious articles of faith.[78] We have to still wait with and see if the US Army will actually let him join and serve by following the judge's decision.

When the public at large does not see any turbaned Sikhs in "uniform," then any turbaned Sikh seems alien. One way to change that is to have many more turbaned Sikhs in "uniform." Then, especially the children will very quickly understand that Sikh Americans are just like any other "American." This change must happen sooner than later if our country prides itself to consider everyone equal under the law. Sikh Americans are not asking for any special favor; rather, we want to put our lives on the line to protect the great values of this nation because we believe deeply in these values.

---

[78] https://www.aclu.org/news/sikh-student-wins-right-join-rotc-beard-long-hair-and-turban

Sikh values and the basic articles of the US Constitution are one and the same.[79] In a post-9/11 era with a shortage of soldiers willing to serve, the US Armed Forces should be soliciting Sikh Americans instead of putting roadblocks up and discriminating against them.

American (Sikh) soldiers

American (Christian or non-Sikh) soldiers

---

[79] Includes the right to bear arms.

Thanks to the amazing foresight and leadership of the newly elected prime minister of Canada, Justin Trudeau,[80] on November 4, 2015, he has included not one but two formally initiated Sikh Canadians in his new cabinet. Lt. Col. Harjit Singh Sajjan holds the post of Minister of National Defense and the Navdeep Singh Bains holds the post of Minister of Innovation, Science and Economic Development.[81] This sends a powerful message of inclusiveness and proper representation not just to Canada but to the entire world. I am optimistic that this phenomenal positive change of societal acceptance in Canada will make a dent and change attitudes in America rapidly.

Lieutenant Colonel Harjit Singh Sajjan of the Canadian
Armed Forces serving in Afghanistan

OVERVIEW OF ADULT BULLYING AGAINST SIKH AMERICANS

Change can be difficult for anyone. Our great founding fathers wrote the constitution for all and everyone who chose to live a life of liberty and freedom, especially the right to practice one's own religion, as long as it does not impinge on anyone else. Religious freedom is one of the primary reasons the Irish, Scots, English, Welsh, German, Dutch, Spanish, Italians, Greek, Polish, Norwegians, Danes, Swedes, Russian, Portuguese, Romanian, Estonians, Lithuanians, Hungarians, Austrians, Serbians, Croatians, Slavs,

---

[80] http://www.nytimes.com/2015/11/05/world/americas/canada-justin-trudeau-sworn-in-as-prime-minister.html?_r=0

[81] http://news.nationalpost.com/news/canada/new-liberal-government-sworn-in-today

Bosnians, Finns, and many others immigrated to America from Western and Eastern Europe in the last few centuries. Yet the constant fear in the subconscious of most European Americans is the possible slow loss of "European American or white cultural values and norms" in case the values of the seemingly "other" becomes popular. One way to slow "it" down is to stomp on "it" in any way you can, and one method is social bullying. This "social bullying" has definitely had its effect on the Sikhs for a very long time, starting with little kids at school to adults within their respective work environment and, in fact, in any public space. Diversity cannot thrive if we as a nation cannot practice it in deed and stop paying lip service to it.

Sikhs were bullied and browbeaten by "white" lynch mobs in Bellingham, Washington, who drove Sikh Americans out of the town as far back as 1907.[82] Well over a hundred years later, 70% of the adult public still does not know who Sikhs are and are in a position to vilify the other because of their own ignorance. It is, indeed, shameful when a sizeable majority of citizens of a particular race and faith group in America choose not to recognize others (un)like them simply because "they" choose to follow their particular faith. The pilgrims who came to America from Europe seemed to have forgotten the primary reason they crossed the Atlantic Ocean was the right to religious freedom which they now deny the slightly newer pilgrims. This kind of hypocrisy is very humanlike and global but requires real effort, maturity, understanding to overcome and be accepting of others, regardless how they look, speak, or dress. I firmly believe that America is made up of good people, but they need to be more educated about others around them who may look different.

A century later, on September 10, 2015, a Sikh American father of two children, 53-year-old Inderjit Singh Mukker, was brutally attacked by a "white" 17-year-old in Darien, Illinois, a suburb of Chicago. According to the *Chicago Tribune*,

---

[82] http://www.bellinghamherald.com/news/local/article22195713.html

Mukker was driving to a grocery store on South Cass Avenue when another driver began yelling at him to "go back to your country," and called him a "terrorist" and "Bin Laden." Mukker pulled over near 69th and Cass to let the other vehicle pass, but the driver pulled in front of him and approached his car. He then reached in and repeatedly punched Mukker in the face. Mukker lost consciousness, was bleeding and had a broken cheekbone. He was taken to the hospital, where he got six stitches.[83]

It took tremendous pressure from the local Sikh American community and faith-based organizations to pursue and make sure that this was treated as a "hate crime" and not just a random incident. Harsimran Kaur of the Sikh Coalition stated, "We are thankful that Robert Berlin and the DuPage County State's Attorney's Office have filed a hate crime charge in this case."[84] The police initially for days did not record this as a hate crime but eventually did, but only after protests and a mass signature campaign. Why are minorities put through the wringer after suffering this kind of bullying is, indeed, problematic.

This kind of hatred is a terrible disease which does not seem to go away and keeps rearing its ugly head at random, creating constant paranoia among Sikh Americans about their own safety 24/7. If a grown adult is not safe while going about their normal daily business, then how can children be safe from violence and bullying?

CONCLUSION

This misinformation and misunderstanding leading to prejudice must stop. Society must rethink new and novel strategies of education for harmony

---

[83] http://www.chicagotribune.com/suburbs/burr-ridge/crime/ct-police-investigate-after-sikh-man-called-terrorist-beaten-in-darien-20150910-story.html September 10, 2015, 5:49 pm

[84] http://www.huffingtonpost.com/entry/sikh-attacked-in-chicago_55f1a8aae4b093be51bdddb3

and coexistence in order to prevent bullying. The beauty of America is in its diversity and respect of each other, regardless of our backgrounds. No one, Sikhs, Muslims or any other faith groups, should be judged based on ignorance, misinformation, and bullied.

POST-9/11: ADULT TO CHILDREN
TRICKLE-DOWN EFFECT OF BIAS

"Do you know what we call opinion in the absence of evidence? We call it prejudice."
Michael Crichton, State of Fear[85]

ATTACK ON AMERICA

Since the attacks on the Twin Towers by a foreign Islamic terrorist group, a section of Americans have been fueling their hatred toward Sikh Americans on a regular basis. Despite the fact that the terrorist hijackers were not Sikh Americans, they were being targeted for discrimination, hate crimes, and bullying.

All the hijackers were clean-shaven men, and none wore turbans. Fifteen out of the nineteen terrorist hijackers of the 9/11 attack on the Twin Towers were from Saudi Arabia, and the rest were from surrounding Middle Eastern countries. Somehow, this translated into going after Sikh Americans, because the media in the US repeatedly showed images of Osama Bin Laden and his cohorts, who wore long beards and turbans. The media relentlessly showed images of turbaned and bearded Middle Eastern men but never addressed the distinction between those bad guys and the Sikh Americans, as well as Sikhs globally. Somehow, the American public made a mistaken connection between Sikh Americans with the images of Osama

---

[85] http://www.goodreads.com/quotes/tag/prejudice

Bin Laden and his evil followers, all due to ignorance of Sikhs, their faith, and their culture. The repercussions of this prejudice were monumental.

FEAR PSYCHOSIS

In order to understand fear psychosis within American society, we have to look at our history. Political power and control is important, therefore, the fear of the other. Humans in power, especially those that have used any and all means to subvert it from others through political chicanery to rule, have always been fearful of the "ruled."

The fear in American society is of what is considered the "other," be it Muslim or Sikh, especially in the charged atmosphere post-9/11. Sikh Americans have been an integral part of society, serving in all arenas of American society for over a hundred years, from being farmers to serving their country. Sikh beliefs are identical to the articles of the US Constitution—namely, ideals like freedom to practice your religion, liberty, justice for all, and the right to bear arms.

Those are the reasons Dr. Navinderdeep Singh Nijher gave his all to help the injured at Ground Zero as a patriotic Sikh American. A fourth-year resident, he set up the first triage center at Ground Zero and helped organize a makeshift morgue in the lobby of the American Express building. Despite all this, he was viciously bullied by other Americans around him while helping the injured during this catastrophe. He was a real American hero.

Dr. Navinderdeep Singh Nijher, MD, in 2001

THE UNSEEN ENEMY: THE BOGEYMAN SYNDROME

America is fortunate that it is surrounded by massive oceans with no enemies sitting on its northern and southern land borders. A country of plenty and blessed with everything a man or woman could ask for to live comfortably. Human nature to find someone to blame and hate whenever there have been any ills within our society or problems beyond our shores that affect us.

During World War I, America's enemies were the Germans, Austrians, Turks, and the Bulgarians; therefore, anyone in America who was of that particular decent was bullied and ostracized. The bullied had to go out of their way to be super citizens in order to show their patriotism and genuine allegiance to America.[86]

During World War II, America's enemies were the Germans, Japanese, and the Italians.[87] However, tens of thousands of Japanese Americans were interned in camps all over the West Coast for the duration of the war, as though they were the enemy. The Japanese Americans were mistreated for years, yet not even a handful of Germans or Italians were interned compared

---

[86] http://www.history-of-american-wars.com/world-war-1-allies.html

[87] http://en.wikipedia.org/wiki/Axis_powers

to the Japanese.[88] In reality, none of the Japanese Americans were found spying for Japan, yet they were bullied!

During the Cold War, which started a few years after the end of World War II, the two major enemies, China and the USSR, neither of whom had fought a war with America, became the prevailing "bogeymen." American society would look down upon anything Russian or Chinese. Finally, with the Berlin Wall coming down, marking the end of the Cold War era, "hating" the "Russian socialist Bear and the Chinese communist Dragon" psychosis got ratcheted down.

Societies everywhere need a focal point to hate in order to feel empowered and unify. Rare is a society which does not coalesce in this manner. America is no different, and as I have shown, our society also has needed a symbol of hate sometimes to feel super patriotic.

The latest "bogeyman" which has been created in the West is "Islam." Anything Islamic or Muslim-like is a free-moving target to be browbeaten by a segment of society and the media. The problem for Sikh Americans is that they are being associated with the bad seeds in the Muslim faith that are not representative of Islam at all. This conflation is the crux of bullying of Sikh American adults, children, and Muslim Americans too.

A recent focus-group study done by Stanford University in conjunction with Sikh American Legal Defense Fund (SALDEF) clearly shows over 70% of the adult public is uninformed and completely ignorant about Sikh Americans. The pent-up rage toward "Islam" is spewed onto Sikh Americans through the similarities of the brown skin, the very visible turbans, and beards.[89] No doubt there have been occasions when the bully clearly knows the faith of the victim. Not every incident is due to ignorance of Islam or the Sikh faith.

---

[88] http://www.archives.gov/research/immigration/enemy-aliens-overview.html

[89] http://saldef.org/policy-research/turban-myths/#.VP3hofzF-So

Case and point is the infamous Oak Creek tragedy in Wisconsin.[90] On August 5, 2012, a white supremacist, Michael Wade, walked into the Oak Creek Gurdwara just before Sunday services began and shot six innocent Sikhs and wounded four others.[91] One of the victims, Satwant Singh Kaleka, the president of the Gurdwara, did put up a fight and tackled the terrorist at the cost of his life. Women and children preparing food in the kitchen hid in closets. Many families were torn apart. This was a national tragedy, and flags across the nation were flown at half-mast. Sometimes bullying the victim is done with the full knowledge of the victim's faith, as was in this case since he was a resident of the local community.

The amount of money spent on the two recent wars[92] against an unseen, unknown bogeyman enemy in two countries on the other side of the planet, the US government could have dispelled ignorance right here in our own backyard through enhanced education, subsidizing college education, keeping jobs here, diversity training, holding seminars, conferences, camps, including possibly creating decent jobs for the people of the countries we attacked, and much more. Instead, the US spent 4.4 trillion dollars and got nothing in return except the ruling elite in the country feeling great that they beat up a bunch of illiterate people in a two third-world countries whose economies were crumbling to begin with. Not to mention the fact that our past governments helped prop up the regimes in both Iraq and Afghanistan. In my opinion, I am not sure if that makes us very brave or mature except for a bullying foreign policy!

Some came five centuries ago and some a century ago. So we should not kid ourselves by claiming one group's superiority over another when, in fact, we are all equal. In fact, bulk of the US population grew with the

---

[90] http://www.nbcnews.com/news/asian-america/oak-creek-community-marks-two-ye ars-sikh-temple-shooting-n171981

[91] http://fox6now.com/2015/08/05/candlelight-vigil-to-mark-three-year-anniversary -of-sikh-temple-shooting/

[92] Wars fought by America in Iraq and Afghanistan, since 9-11.

influx of Europeans in the early part of the last century due to the two great World Wars and other economic woes in several countries across Europe.

In order to eradicate the effects of the bogeyman syndrome, we need to create a cohesive society which respects diversity. Education is critical so we know more about each other.

RESPONSIBILITY OF THE MEDIA

The media in our country has the most freedom to write on any topic thanks to our wonderful democratic institutions. However, media has the power to be a bully too. Powerful images are critical in media portrayal. However, the fact underlying the image is not always accurate. Sikh American portrayal in the US media has made these erroneous connections of terrorism encouraging prejudice, stereotyping, categorizing, and, ultimately, leading to bullying and sometimes death.

This is an issue which can be tackled by a sensitive and responsible press. Unfortunately, the overall numbers of Sikh Americans do not matter, and/or their financial clout has not been used in a way to signal their displeasure of being ignored and only being covered when either there is a tragedy, albeit being covered in a limited way or, on many occasions, showing a "turbaned Sikh" while covering a story of a Muslim. This makes it kind of double jeopardy and does not bode well for people of either faith.

The case of the horrific Oak Creek Gurdwara shooting by a "white terrorist," Michael Wade, in Wisconsin is a perfect example of problematic coverage of Sikh Americans in the media. Issue of coverage included scanty coverage a little too late, lack of knowledge of Sikhs, and how race affects media coverage.

The *New York Times* described the Oak Creek tragedy coverage by the media as scanty: "As a result, the massacre in Oak Creek is treated as a tragedy for Sikhs in America rather than a tragedy for all Americans."[93]

---

[93] https://www.quora.com/Why-is-there-not-as-much-US-media-attention-to-the-Sikh-Temple-Shooting-in-Wisconsin

Nadra Nittle of the Maynard Media Institute on Structural Inequity said it best. In her opinion,

> One question that must be examined is whether coverage of Sikhs was too late in coming. Did lack of knowledge about their religion contribute to the victims being targeted in the attack and previous incidents of violence across the country? If so, the mainstream media must share in the blame for not educating the public. Recent coverage has demonstrated clearly that the media failed to report on bigotry historically faced by Sikhs in the United States, say practitioners of the faith. Sikhs also believe that reckless imagery in the media after the 9/11 terrorist attacks fueled misconceptions about them and their religion.[94]

Knowledge of the other plays a significant role in media coverage. According to *US News*,[95] "[P]eople who shape discourse in this country by and large aren't Sikhs and don't know many if any Sikhs."[96] Robert Wright writes in *The Atlantic*, "They can imagine their friends and relatives—and themselves—being at a theater watching a batman movie; they can't imagine being in a Sikh temple."[97]

Race is factor in media coverage. Danielle Christenson, in her thesis, "Victim Worthiness: The Effect of Media Coverage on the Portrayal of Homicide Victims," stated, "Race does affect the coverage of crime. White victims are favored over minority victims."[98] This is simply a reality since there are no visible Sikh American journalists to affect change at the moment.

---

[94] http://mije.org/mmcsi/criminal-justice/media-may-share-responsibility-sikh-temple-shootings

[95] Teresa Welsh in *US News* stated on August 8, 2012

[96] http://www.usnews.com/opinion/articles/2012/08/08/is-the-media-undercovering-the-wisconsin-sikh-temple-shooting

[97] http://www.usnews.com/opinion/articles/2012/08/08/is-the-media-undercovering-the-wisconsin-sikh-temple-shooting

[98] http://vc.bridgew.edu/cgi/viewcontent.cgi?article=1278&context=undergrad_rev

However, this does that allow journalists and the media to be remiss of their ethical responsibility of unbiased and balanced coverage of all stories.

CONCLUSION

The perpetual fear created by the media's sensational portrayal of the other has conditioned the general public to be on high alert 24/7. This leads to suspicion of the other and constant stress. Our government must take some responsibility in finding ways to balance the fine line between informing the public of any threat without creating paranoia, which may lead to hateful outcomes against minorities.

MEDIA PORTRAYAL OF SIKHS

"Media, like an un-mannered master, manipulates the meek minds."
Junaid e Mustafa[99]

TURBANS AND BEARDS IN HOLLYWOOD CINEMA

For more than a century, Hollywood has vilified the Arabs, who happen to be predominantly Muslim. The overwhelmingly white producers purposely never see beyond their noses when it comes to the anti-Muslim hate production. Continuously denigrating a very large ethnic/religious group is going to create animosity, leading to violence eventually.[100] Conditioning of stereotypical Arab Muslims has encouraged deep-rooted racism, which then becomes conflated with the Sikhs since they are the closest reality to the cinematic evil turban.

Since 1896, there have been over 1,000 movies made by Hollywood that have visible Arab/Muslim characters. Only 26 had a positive portrayal, 52 had a neutral portrayal, but over 900 had varying degrees of negative portrayal of Arab/Muslim characters.[101] This continuous conditioning of society has undoubtedly skewed the mindset of most European Americans. I, for one, and my parents have never seen a turbaned Arab in America; therefore, whenever a visible Sikh like me is walking down the school

---

[99] http://www.goodreads.com/quotes/tag/media-bias

[100] https://www.youtube.com/watch?v=lugFgJn9krI

[101] Reel Bad Arabs by Dr.Jack Shaheen, How Hollywood vilifies a people, Annals of American Academy of Political and Social Science, Pages 171-193

hallways or on Main Street America, the instant image of the cinematic turbaned bad guy flashes across the brains of the masses who see me as the "'other." The reaction is instantaneous but varies due to the societal norms, constraints of the law, and the place. Sometimes, while I have been watching a movie with family or friends and sitting in the front section inside a theater, someone in the audience will yell a racial epithet based on what is on the movie screen. This is invisible bullying!

It seems, in my experience, that a movie with Arab/Muslim characters, but especially turbaned characters, brings out the worst in some people who will react instantly and lash out at the nearest person who they think is the most closely related to the cinematic evil guy.

Facial profiling by all animators in America is done with certain traits in mind that are then exaggerated to define a particular ethnic or religious group all based on the typically white mindset of others.[102] Arabs will be characteristically shown as mostly bearded, ugly, bad guys, while white Americans shown in very masculine, handsome, and flattering ways.

MEDIA PORTRAYAL: CONDITIONING FOR BULLYING

It is rare for the media to accurately portray a Sikh. Again and again, Sikhs have been mentioned and assumed to be Muslims. Sikhs are also mentioned as a sect of Hinduism in dozens upon dozens of books, which is false. Many times, the news is about the Middle East or a Muslim and the picture being flashed across the TV screen is a Sikh. Even though someone might reach out to the media for a retraction, the damage is already done. There is fear within every Sikh, because of the negative publicity and the more serious repercussions that follow many times. The only unknown question is when and where the bullying may occur. From my perspective, the Sikh Americans should be the most paranoid people, since the majority can subject us to vilifications anytime anywhere without any warning whatsoever.

It seems particularly disturbing that the US Department of Defense has been financing Hollywood movies that vilify Arabs and Muslims over

---

[102] http://tvtropes.org/pmwiki/pmwiki.php/Main/FacialProfiling

the years.[103] This negative portrayal of Muslims and Sikhs is a contributing factor to bullying by society.

Nadine Nabir, a scholar with the Barnard Center for Research on Women, uses the term "internment of the psyche" in one of her research papers.[104] This is very poignant as it explains the predicament of the Sikh school-going child in America today. If a Sikh child is made to feel as an outsider by his/her peer group and the educators continuously, regardless of the level of bullying, it makes the child feel as though he/she is under siege and cannot properly blossom to their potential. This type of situation, once created, can only have negative ramifications. In order to produce good, wholesome, able-bodied citizens, this internment through bullying must stop.

Just like names signifying an "Arab/Middle Eastern/Muslim" identity reduce particular men and boys to foreign or alien and assumed to be "terrorists," in the same manner any turban-wearing boy or man is immediately looked at as the other, even though someone like me who is born in the good ole USA. The constant fear for a Muslim American, especially post-9/11, is one of internal incarceration that is emotive and manifested into the fear that, at any moment, one could be bullied, harassed, beaten up, picked up, locked up, or made to disappear. This same extraordinary stress is genuinely felt by every Sikh American as the self-defensive paranoia of the "white European American" trying to hurt them (Sikh Americans) anywhere and everywhere is very real.

As a teenager in middle school and in high school, the passing whispering taunts of "Osama," "towelhead," "raghead," and many other religious, insensitive racial epithets are very common and regular to hear for a Sikh American youngster across the hallways and schoolyards of America. Can anyone imagine similar bullying being reversed and targeted onto the "European American" kids, especially girls? Many would be diagnosed

---

[103] https://www.youtube.com/watch?v=m-OAUwCnBtg Lamis Deek, US Human Rights Attorney, May 7, 2012

[104] http://sfonline.barnard.edu/immigration/naber_03.htm Nadine Naber, "Look, Mohammed the Terrorist Is Coming!" Cultural Racism, Nation-Based Racism, and the Intersectionality of Oppressions after 9/11. Page 3

with "post-traumatic stress disorder" (PTSD) and would stop going to school completely, not to mention the bullies getting into serious trouble. Children like me have to develop a thick skin, and our parents have to work ten times harder to find ways to protect us from the power of the "majority" so that we are able to withstand a higher degree of bullying than others.

The American media, like any media, seems to thrive on sensationalism, and what better way than to condition the minds of all Americans to make them paranoid of anyone who does not fit the "good old blond boy" mold? American media has done a good job of perpetuating a "media generated" caricature of what a terrorist should look like and then used that "bogeyman" to beat anyone they want, including entire populations and communities outside and inside the US. This is the most insidious and dangerous rise of media generated "knowledge" which has dehumanized many religious minorities to the extent that changing the status quo has become a monumental challenge.

As Salah Masri, director of one of the largest mosques in San Francisco, explained,

> I know this man who is a peaceful Tunisian Muslim that dresses in white robe with a long beard. He is extremely quiet and polite. He is a good engineer. He is an Internet web designer. After September 11, we didn't see him at the masjid for a long time. When we asked about him, it turned out he didn't feel comfortable changing his clothes or shaving his beard so he decided to stay home. Some people didn't want to look Muslim. I know people who dyed their hair blond. One of them was a Turkish guy who dyed his hair blond because he thought he looked Arab or Middle Eastern. We had many cases of people shaving their beards or people who stopped attending

the mosque. But why dye your hair? He still looked Middle Eastern with it![105]

STEREOTYPING SIKHS

Sikh Americans, especially males and some females, cover their head with the religiously mandated turbans and are extremely distinguished, yet their persona is associated with the media-generated "bad guy Arab." This negative image seems to be seared in the minds of the majority of the European American, Hispanic American, and many African American people. The stares, stepping aside, flipping the finger, yelling, screaming, pushing, shoving, violent assault, and, finally, murder has put the Sikh Americans on a 24/7 vigilance about their personal safety from their co-citizens in the freest country in the world.

The fear was so intense immediately after September 11, 2001, that many Sikhs did not even go to work, some for a few days and others for a longer period. Many Sikh adults removed any religiously mandated manifestations of their faith overnight; others who were self-employed wore baseball caps to work to take the turban out of sight. The hypersensitivity and vigilance does take its toll on the mental and physical health every time a visible Sikh is out in the public domain, which is daily.

The conflation of "looking Muslim" with "looking Arab or Middle Eastern" exemplifies agreement among many in the US that do not distinguish between "Arabs," "Middle Easterners," "Muslims," and "Sikhs" but construct an image of an "Arab/Middle Eastern/Muslim look." Anybody who closely resembles the mainstream commercial media's "Arab/Middle Eastern/Muslim look" is particularly vulnerable to federal government policies and harassment on the streets 24/7. I wonder sometimes why has the media spared "Jesus Christ" from all this when he happened to be from the Middle East and completely Middle Eastern–looking! Was it only because

---

[105] http://sfonline.barnard.edu/immigration/naber_05.htm Dark-Skinned, Bearded Terrorists, and the "Queery-ing" of "Muslim Masculinities" by Nadine Naber

the media in the US is predominantly white and Christian, therefore, sees Jesus as one of their own and not the adopted "other"?

DOUBLE STANDARDS

The federal government went after "the European American version" of what a terrorist supposedly looks like. He was dark, Middle Eastern, and had a full beard. He was the typical terrorist-looking guy—or the guy portrayed by all major TV channels as the terrorist. In America, by default, it would be a Sikh American because they are the only ones who are religiously mandated to wear turbans and fit the rest of the supposed media profile.

Homeland Security in particular, even today, after more than 14 years post-9/11, has frequent complaints by Sikh travelers who get harassed while going through security. This special humiliation for Sikhs has not changed but rather is the rule today. All Sikhs, at a very minimum, are given two options when they go through security screening across the US. First, the Sikh passenger can run both hands over their turban in full public view and then stretch their open palms to be chemically swabbed and tested for bomb-type chemical material. It is akin to asking any woman to run her hands over her own chest in public and then swab her hands, checking for chemicals related to a bomb. The second option for a Sikh passenger is to have the homeland security officer physically feel the passenger's turban in public or private, depending on the officer's discretion. Again, this is akin to having stranger feeling a woman or man's privates in full public view. This continued degrading humiliation of Sikh American citizens is outrageous because they are being profiled because of the beards and turbans. Since September 11, 2001, there has not been a single incident where a Sikh American was found with a weapon with intent to harm anyone.

While traveling by air, I have never observed a Christian Catholic nun ever being asked to do the same self-examination or being physically examined by a Homeland Security official, while I get the special treatment. Security checks are visible since most screenings are done in full public view. There appears to be a double standard.

While being on the subject of Catholic nuns, as long as they are white, they are "terrorist proof," but the minute they are brown skinned with non-European sounding names, they can become moving targets too. One such incident took place in June 2004 when four Catholic nuns were stopped, harassed, and humiliated on their second leg of a flight originating in Wichita, Kansas, heading to San Francisco, California. While the plane taxied, ready to take off from Fort Worth/Dallas airport, these four Carmelite, California–based nuns were interrogated, taken back to the airport, deplaned, and their baggage scrutinized. All this because the nuns were dark-skinned women and happened to be of Indian descent. Even though they had Christian names, alarm bells went off in the minds of airport security because they have been conditioned to think a certain way thanks to the media brainwashing.[106] To add further insult to injury, American Airlines sent them a letter of apology with the reason, stating "an unusual odor" in the cabin as the reason for the plane's return to the gate: "Inasmuch as this odor seemed to emanate from your row on the plane, you were afforded a bit more attention than the other passengers." A situation like this should have been handled very tactfully; instead, it showed the influence of the media on airline personnel. Most people are not looking for any special treatment in such cases but do expect sensitivity and respect as human beings.

Timothy McVeigh, the infamous bomber who blew up an entire federal building in downtown Oklahoma City, Oklahoma, on April 19, 1995, which killed 168 and grievously injured over 600 Americans, was a "terrorist," but not once has he ever been mentioned anywhere in the American media as a "white, European-American Christian terrorist" ever.[107] The question is why not? Whereas, Muslims and Sikhs can be labeled based on their faith, even for the slightest infraction so easily by the white-majority media.

---

[106] http://www.wrmea.org/2004-june/four-nuns-among-six-passengers-removed-from-american-airlines-flight.html

[107] http://www.fbi.gov/about-us/history/famous-cases/oklahoma-city-bombing

This hypocritical double standard is exactly what is causing a large part of the effect on children, who end up bullying their peers who happen to be of a minority ethnic or religious group. Children are not dumb; in fact, today's kids are far wiser than a generation ago. When school children see the hypocrisy of the adults played out in society through bullying, they emulate the same behaviors. Therefore, adults need to reset their moral compasses, rethink their biases, and educate themselves in order to make a more harmonious society while respecting each other.

NIGHTMARE OF FLYING FOR SIKH AMERICANS

My father travels quite a bit and has to deal with the public, so has many stories to tell before 9/11 but much scarier ones after 9/11.

I remember once my father was travelling to San Francisco, CA, from Philadelphia, PA, in November 2012. He was standing in a long line waiting to go through security when a big "white man with a Texan hat" standing in front of him rudely asked him if he was not going to remove that thing on his head. My father loudly told him to mind his own business and that he was not going to remove that thing for him or the security and complained to the police at the airport. A situation such as this is outright bigotry. The adult bully is invisible since pretty much everyone around him is white and quiet, while the bullied "other" is humiliated, harassed, stressed, and shaken up. The system is biased to a degree, yes, but varies from place to place.

In two of the three incidents of bigotry where my father had to call the police since 9/11, the police actually told him the perpetrator "did not mean what he said" and tried to downplay the seriousness of the bias incidents in two towns of Southern New Jersey. On the other hand, the police actually stopped my father while walking through the neighborhood one evening because someone called the police, stating there was a strange man walking on the road, so my father had to identify himself and give a reason for his evening walk.

For a few years after 2001, there was a huge drop in travel by Sikh Americans within the US because of the unusually high level of scrutiny and humiliation they had to go through for no reason other than standing up for their own faith. "Sikh Americans have stopped flying altogether in the months and, in some cases, years after 9/11 to avoid potential problems."[108] In the summer of 2007, my 84-year-old granduncle, a retired professor emeritus of civil engineering from Ohio State University, chose to drive 1,800 miles to attend a funeral in Vancouver, Canada, from central California simply to avoid being humiliated at the airport because of the turban. This is a man who has worked on defense contracts all his life and is a patriotic American. Can anyone imagine not being able to freely fly and move around in your country because your co-citizens might hurt you simply for looking different?

Some of the responsibility lies with the government to educate the public, and there are many ways that can be achieved. Highway billboards, bus billboards, TV ads, internet media sites, diversity training for all government personnel in any capacity are some of the ways the government can bring some measure of reducing the public's paranoia in reducing the bullying against Sikh Americans.

Recent research done by Stanford University clearly shows that men who have beards coupled with dark skin were among those most severely concerned for their safety—particularly if they wore religious forms of dress perceived to be associated with Islam. In several focus studies, when a turbaned man was shown holding a bottle, the vast majority of "white" observers saw a gun or weapon from their recalled memory.[109] Over 70 percent of the responders of this 2013 study did not know the correct faith of a turbaned man, who was actually a Sikh. This astoundingly high ignorance factor on the part of the general public and, particularly, white European American society is cause for concern.

Sikh American teenagers even designed and came out with a tee shirt which had the map of the United States with all the major airports in it,

---

[108] *Civil Rights in Wartime: The Post-9/11 Sikh Experience*, Dawinder Singh Sidhu & Neha Singh Gohil (2009) [214P] ISBN:978-0-7546-7553-2 www.ashgate.com; Page 161

[109] Turban Myths by Stanford University and SALDEF, an in-depth focuses group study on the awareness about the "turban" done in 2013.

and across the front, the caption stated, "100% randomly searched at the following airports."[110]

A popular T-shirt worn by many Sikh Americans

For example, in 2007, the Transportation Security Administration (TSA) made an overnight decision to place turbans on a list of "suspicious headwear" that must be secondarily searched at US airports.[111] It is strange that the turban is perceived to be a "dangerous object" in the eyes of Homeland Security, yet baggy pants, any kind of loose clothing, particularly the "habit" of a Catholic nun, are not? Again, this is a combination of many factors but primarily ignorance and paranoia. If items can be hid inside a turban, supposedly, then anyone could hide items within body cavities and elsewhere. Therefore, "everyone" should be strip-searched using the suspicion excuse.

Finally, the four most common head coverings for Orthodox Jews, which would, in some way, cover their foreheads, are the tefillin, the yarmulke, the hat/shtreimel, and the tallit. Objects and materials could be carried by the

---

[110] http://rootsgear.com/collections/t-shirts/products/100-randomly-searched

[111] *Civil Rights in Wartime: The Post-9/11 Sikh Experience*, Dawinder Singh Sidhu & Neha Singh Gohil (2009) [214P] ISBN:978-0-7546-7553-2 www.ashgate.com; Page 187

above-mentioned religious Christians and Jews, but most are not treated the same way as I am at the airports, from personal experience.

Sikhs who wear turbans were repeatedly misidentified as Muslims (and in some cases killed) points to the ways in which a range of signifiers can stand in as symbols of an "Arab/Middle Eastern/Muslim look." Cases such as these redefine dominant US distinctions between those who are with us and those who are with the terrorists by rendering particular kinds of "subjects" not only as unassimilable or "fundamentally foreign and anti-pathetic to modern European American society and cultures" but also as threatening to national security and, therefore, legitimate targets of violence and harassment. What about the rights of any Muslim American citizen to be safe and not have their faith considered less than equal? These are serious issues our society must deal with today. Procrastinating while innocents, regardless of their faith, are bullied is not an option.

Moreover, cases in which Sikh American men considered shaving their beards, cutting their hair, or avoiding attending their Gurdwaras illustrate the tremendous societal peer pressure put on religious minorities to conform because the media has created a "bogeyman syndrome" and conditioned the public into thinking that any turbaned persons are "potential terrorists" who are also perceived as violent "crazy Muslims," therefore, are open season to bullying. Again, no one should be subject to bullying and vilification, regardless of their faith.

CONSEQUENCES OF NEGATIVE PORTRAYAL IN PRINT MEDIA

One of the chapters on "Social Psychology" in my AP Psychology high school book contained an entire page focused on the negative portrayal of a Sikh American man picked up by the police authorities on September 12, 2001, a day after the horrific 9/11 terrorist attack on the World Trade Center in New York City. Social conditioning is so pervasive that it permeates every nook and cranny of especially "white society."[112] Sher Singh,

---

[112] *Understanding Psychology*, 10th edition by Charles G.Moris, Albert A.Maisto Pearson Education, Inc., 2014 ISBN-10: 0-205-98618-8, Page 457

"formally initiated" into the Sikh faith and an (IT) professional, was traveling via the Amtrak train on the Boston–Washington, DC, corridor when some stranger called the police and got him arrested simply for looking suspicious because he was wearing a turban and sported a beard. He was publicly humiliated by being arrested, dragged through the media, then taken to court but eventually all charges being dropped. The scene of Sher Singh being arrested was flashed across the world television screens from every major television network and is seared into the memories of every Sikh American watching that day very painfully.

Sher Singh being illegally arrested and bullied by the authorities,
September 12, 2001

On the other hand, all non-Sikhs, especially European Americans, became hyper sensitive to turbans and beards, adding to their fear of the unknown enemy. Yet the dichotomy is that none of the 9/11 hijackers were turban-wearing; rather, they looked very much like any "East European American" (un)clean-shaven, and none even remotely looked like a "Sikh." Furthermore, there was no way of telling what faith they belonged to other than their very Muslim names. In fact, fifteen of the 9/11 hijackers were from Saudi Arabia and the other four were from Lebanon, United Arab Emirates, and Egypt.[113]

None of these countries were attacked by the US to date, yet the first casualty of the 9/11 aftermath was a Sikh American. On September 16, 2001, Balbir Singh Sodhi was murdered in broad daylight while Sodhi was outside his Chevron gas station planting flowers in Phoenix, Arizona.[114] What followed has been a continuous barrage of bullying and "other-ing" of law-abiding Sikh American citizenry simply for looking different. Furthermore, a racist in the San Francisco Bay area, also killed Sodhi's other brother while he was driving his taxi. The media has done an injustice by ignoring and improperly covering crimes against thousands of Sikh Americans by their co-citizens.

To this day, Sher Singh never received an apology from the law enforcement officers for being bullied or the court for the humiliating illegal arrest and misguided paranoia of the authorities. The social conditioning of human beings in making preconceived opinions of others who are unfamiliar to the majority is known as "social cognition."

There was a very interesting and humorous response to "turban-phobia" during an online discussion recently, which is as follows:

> Ryan Carr: "Am I racist if I feel uncomfortable about a guy with a turban on my plane because this isn't okay with me."
>
> Ashishpal Singh: "I know what you mean I get really uncomfortable when I see a white man walk into a movie theatre or an elementary school."[115]

There have been well over a 1,000 registered incidents, all hate crimes against Sikh Americans, in the last fourteen years, but the actual number

---

[113] http://usatoday30.usatoday.com/news/world/2002/02/06/saudi.htm

[114] http://www.nytimes.com/2001/09/17/us/sikh-owner-of-gas-station-is-fatally-shot-in-rampage.html

[115] http://www.vox.com/2014/8/6/5974305/this-is-the-best-possible-response-when-someone-says-they-dont-want

would be ten times more. Very few of these actually were dealt as "hate crimes" but were instead handled as "incidents." Dealing with any bureaucratic system is time consuming, and the police department is even more stressful. The traumatized and bullied first-generation Sikh American is going to be circumspect about complaining to the police because of the prior experience from the old country[116] where the police are corrupt. Since the vast majority of the profiling/bullying complaints go unreported, underreported, and unregistered, statistics are skewed and understated. This is also part of the problem that causes the media not to highlight this pervasive bullying issue as much as it should be.

The three registered police complaints by my father from 2001–2007 of hate crime incidents against him never got registered as "hate crimes" but only as "terrorist threats." He followed through with two and won. He has had several incidents prior to 2001.

VIOLENCE IN VIDEO GAMES AND MOVIES IN GENERAL

Violence and its role in bullying is complex in itself, but there is no getting around the fact that pervasive violence in the vast majority of video games catering to the 11-plus-year-old's mental condition while molding the minds to a certain degree. This is affecting the way children view violence in general but especially toward others who are different than themselves.[117] Dr. Bruce Bartholow, associate professor of psychology at the University of Missouri, states that "a single exposure to violent video games would not lead to violence, but this desensitization can occur over time." Further, he argues, "I believe that there is a real reliable link between exposure to violent video games and aggression in the short-term." The reality is that children are getting exposed to these violent games continuously and it is rare that they play only once and stop.

---

[116] The police in India are not only biased but also completely corrupt; rather than helping will create more trouble typically, therefore normal people avoid going to the police.

[117] http://www.cbsnews.com/news/violent-video-games-and-mass-violence-a-complex-link/

Therefore, I would argue that the desensitization is widespread, which plays into bullying in various ways—not to mention the very visible Arab headgear and beards on the bad guys in most of the video games being played in the Western Hemisphere, albeit globally. If children are being conditioned a certain way, even though unconsciously right under their very well-meaning parents, one can only imagine the level of hysteria going through the juveniles' heads when adults are having a dialogue while the children are listening in.

A very fascinating article by Vit Sisler called "Digital Arabs: Representation in Video Games" brings out the subtleties and the negative effects of demonizing all Muslim "head gear – turban wearing" Arabs with a single brush.[118] By creating a holier-than-thou "us" and worse-than-the-devil "them," the general public and, especially, teenagers fall victim to this type of social conditioning since video gaming is now a daily occurrence in most American households. By creating the hostile "other" bogeyman, most in North America and Western Europe absorb the images and eventually create a very adverse perception of anyone with a brownish skin tone, possibly bearded, and especially anyone with a "turban." Recent surveys and research done in America and Europe shows the following, according to Vit Sisler:

1. The dominant discourses overwhelmingly present most followers of Islam as a threat;[119]
2. Islam is likely to be linked with terrorism;[120]
3. The representation of "ordinary Muslims" is marginalized;[121]
4. A conflictual framework dominates.[122]

---

[118] http://www.digitalislam.eu/article.do?articleId–1704 Sisler, Vit. "Digital Arabs: Representation in Video Games." *European Journal of Cultural Studies*. Vol. 11, No. 2, SAGE Publications, 2008, pp. 203–220. ISSN: 1367-5494.

[119] (Hafez, 2000; Karim, 2006; Poole, 2006; Richardson, 2004);

[120] (Karim, 2006; Manning, 2006; Miller, 2006)

[121] (Richardson, 2006);

[122] (Karim, 2006; Manning, 2006)

It is extremely rare to find anyone in America wearing a turban and who also happens to be a Muslim/Arab, especially in public. The overwhelming likelihood of that turbaned person being of the Sikh faith is exceedingly high. In this very corrosive cauldron, the turban-wearing Sikh American gets caught in the crossfire and gets the sharp end of the society's big stick for no fault at all other than being perceived as the "other" thanks to the prolific video game designers whose sole aim is to make money, and any political/religious correctness or sensitivity be damned.

BOLLYWOOD ENCOURAGES NEGATIVE PORTRAYAL OF SIKHS

Bollywood has also penetrated the American family room with its negative portrayal of Sikhs. Thanks to cable television and YouTube, more and more Americans watch Bollywood movies for their entertainment value. Unlike movies from other countries, Bollywood movies are a unique genre. Most movies, like the ones made in Hollywood, have separate genres of comedy, tragedy, drama, action, or art, but Bollywood has a unique twist. They have all the genres rolled into one, called "masala movie," meaning "spice movie." One of the spices added in these movies is to mock Sikhs.[123]

A recent report in a major national newspaper of India, *The Hindu*, had statistics showing that between 2013–2014, out of 285 movies, there were only six movies where upper caste Hindus actors played the roles of turbaned Sikhs.[124] What was missing from the report was whether the roles were shown in a positive or a negative role. From my research on those six movies, two had an overall positive Sikh lead character role, but the other four movies made a mockery out of the Sikh character, showing them in very poor light. This does not include the hundreds of other movies which have extremely tiny roles, while the role is viciously patronizing the Sikh persona and a footnote in the overall movies.

---

[123] The most powerful politicians in India are overwhelmingly upper caste Hindus.

[124] http://m.thehindu.com/news/national/in-bollywood-storylines-remain-backward-on-caste/article7362298.ece

Sikhs are portrayed as stupid, antiheroes, antinationals, treacherous, as terrorists, and much more. This skewed information feeds into negative perceptions of Sikhs. This sets the stage for bullying of not only adults but also children. Even Sikh children are bullied by making them objects of cheap jokes in movies.[125]

MISLABELING AND REDIRECTING RADICALIZATION

My research shows that there is radicalization of some individuals from the Muslim faith, but they are fewer compared to the radicalization of individuals from the Christian faith that are overwhelmingly of European American extraction in the US. The question of the "enemy within" is an enigma. Whose perspective are we using to describe the "enemy"? For example, a Muslim American of Lebanese descent may be mortally afraid of all white Americans, considering them to be his enemy. A Christian European American of German descent may be mortally afraid of all brown-skinned men with beards and considers them his enemy. The official government narrative called the "war on terror" seems to capture only Muslims in their dragnet, largely ignoring the homegrown terror of the "white supremacists" that quietly are running rampant beneath the radar and within our nation's borders. The hypocrisy and double standards by our government, which is largely run by older Christian European American men and some women, is troublesome and causes serious fallout for the "other."

According to Nidhi Parkash, "The report is based on court documents, wire service, and news stories. It looks at 'lethal terrorist incidents' with a clear ideological motivation since 2001. Forty-eight (48) people were killed in nineteen (19) terrorist attacks by white supremacists, anti-government activists, and other extremists classified as right wing."[126] It is amusing that "white terrorists" are defined as right wing, but any "right wingers of Middle Eastern descent" are labeled as terrorists! There was a similar report on BBC

---

[125] "Kuch Kuch Hota Hai" and "Khoobsoorat."

[126] http://fusion.net/story/155989/report-more-americans-have-been-killed-by-white-supremacists-than-muslim-extremists-since-911/

in the summer of 2015 reporting the same issue and questioning the under reporting of the "white" homegrown terrorism. The report further states, "That means that in total, the number of Americans killed by non-Muslim extremists since 9/11 is nearly twice the number killed by Muslim extremists, based on the New America study. But what is classified as extremist ideology and terrorism remains difficult to pin down."[127] According to the *New York Times* report on June 24, 2015, under the heading of "Homegrown Extremists Tied to Deadlier Toll Than Jihadists in US. Since 9/11," Scott Shane states, "A survey to be published this week asked 382 police and sheriff's departments nationwide to rank the three biggest threats from violent extremism in their jurisdiction. About 74 percent listed 'antigovernment violence,' while 39 percent listed 'Al Qaeda-inspired' violence, according to the researchers, Charles Kurzman of the University of North Carolina and David Schanzer of Duke University."[128]

There is an eye-opening statement made by John G. Horgan in the same report, who studies terrorism at the University of Massachusetts, Lowell, MA, who said, "The mismatch between public perceptions and actual cases has become steadily more obvious to scholars."[129] Further, "There's an acceptance now of the idea that the threat from jihadi terrorism in the United States has been overblown."[130] Dr. Horgan said, "And there's a belief that the threat of right-wing, antigovernment violence has been underestimated."[131]

The real bullies live in plain sight, yet the rhetoric does not stop. The war against terror, without boundaries, simply continues draining our

---

[127] http://fusion.net/story/155989/report-more-americans-have-been-killed-by-white-supremacists-than-muslim-extremists-since-911/

[128] http://www.nytimes.com/2015/06/25/us/tally-of-attacks-in-us-challenges-perceptions-of-top-terror-threat.html?_r=1

[129] http://www.nytimes.com/2015/06/25/us/tally-of-attacks-in-us-challenges-perceptions-of-top-terror-threat.html?_r=1

[130] http://www.nytimes.com/2015/06/25/us/tally-of-attacks-in-us-challenges-perceptions-of-top-terror-threat.html?_r=1

[131] http://www.nytimes.com/2015/06/25/us/tally-of-attacks-in-us-challenges-perceptions-of-top-terror-threat.html?_r=1

country's resources while creating a climate of fear and hate not just within but also outside our borders.

For a country to become great, enormous energy needs to be spent on educating everyone not just in their particular field to get a job but also learning about world history, religions, cultures, and general societal etiquette as the America I know is not a melting pot, which some want it to be, but a multicultural mosaic where everyone's heritage can be proudly shared, equally respected, and rejoiced.

CONCLUSION

In the post-9/11 backlash, the category "Arab, Muslim, South Asian" has been incorporated into liberal US multicultural dialogues. Consider, for example, diversity initiatives that have operated to single out Arabs, Muslims, and, actually, Sikhs as the only "targeted communities" in the post-9/11 time frame. Such "targeting" has reinforced within these same religious communities that there is institutionalized racism, producing oppression by marginalizing them and, thereby, excluding them. Some of the immigrant policies were changed quickly due to the Patriot Act of 2001 through the Bill HR4437 of 2006 as a Latino/border issue, but this did affect all Arabs, Muslims, and South Asians as it intensified a vicious anti-immigrant backlash. Among the so-called South Asian category, the overwhelming section who are still being bullied are the Sikhs.

Arabs, Muslims, Middle Easterners, Sikhs, and other communities have been historically targeted by racism, colonization, and state violence in their previous homelands and now in their new homeland. "Many racial justice activists and scholars have agreed that survivors of 9/11-related federal government policies and incidents of harassment in the public sphere tended to be Arab, Muslim, and Sikhs, but that this is not an isolated case of group marginalization."[132]

---

[132] http://sfonline.barnard.edu/immigration/naber_05.htm Dark-Skinned, Bearded Terrorists, and the "Queery-ing" of "Muslim Masculinities" by Nadine Naber

The bulk of incidents due to religious racism have occurred mostly against male Sikh Americans because they are extremely distinguished because of their religiously mandated turbans and beards. Most male Muslim Americans are not distinguishable on sight unless they choose to have beards without mustaches. Muslim women are also only distinguishable if they choose to wear the hijab, burqa, or niqab in public since it is not religiously mandated.

Unfortunately, misinformation and misunderstanding of a "Sikh" being an "Arab Muslim" in the minds of the bully is the cause of most of the misery. In some cases, the bully is knowledgeable about the faith of a Sikh but chooses to be a bigoted bully regardless. Ignorance and the irresponsibility of the media have further caused bullying against different religious personas. No one has the right to bully—Sikh, Muslim or anyone else—because of the person's faith, ethnicity, color, heritage, and any other distinguishing marker.

CURRENT BULLYING STATISTICS FOR SIKH AMERICAN CHILDREN

"Life is a fight, but not everyone's a fighter. Otherwise,
bullies would be an endangered species."
Andrew Vachss, Terminal[133]

MY PERSONAL BULLYING SURVEY

Surveys have been done to address the issue of bullying by Sikh American organizations, like Sikh Coalition and SALDEF, in the past several years. The surveys have been eye-openers for many inside and outside the affected community. These organizations have of worked diligently to educate and highlight the issues over the years in order to reduce bullying in schools. The last large bullying survey was done in 2007. As time passes, attitudes could change. My goal was to find out what the state of bullying was in 2015? I personally wanted to find out if, in fact, Sikh American children in schools were being bullied.

I wanted to find out how bullying affected Sikh American children and see if there has been any change in education regarding Sikh Americans in schools. I designed a survey to find the answers to my questions. The questions were designed with the input of a few seasoned professionals so that they could be answered easily by all age groups and in a short time

---

[133] http://www.goodreads.com/quotes/tag/bullying

frame. Getting a survey done by a school-going child is not as simple as I thought. Regardless of the situation, bullied or not, children need an explanation and prodding just to complete a survey.

I spent several months completing the bullying survey. It was an uphill task. I was studying for my 11th grade finals and preparing for the SAT like many of my peers during the spring of 2015. The work took longer due to the holidays and the summer vacation. During this timeframe, in summer I traveled to a few gurdwaras and summer camps in New Jersey and New York. Nevertheless, I managed and did my best to complete the surveys in a timely fashion, under the circumstances, with the help of adult members within the community.

Statistics were gathered by using a system similar to "survey monkey" through the gurdwaras, Sikh camps, and individual children.[134]

Even though Sikh Americans reside in practically every state in the union, this survey was only sent to 60-plus gurdwaras in the states of Alabama, California, Colorado, Connecticut, Florida, Georgia, Illinois, Louisiana, Massachusetts, Michigan, Mississippi, Missouri, North Carolina, New Hampshire, New Jersey, Nevada, New York, Ohio, Pennsylvania, South Carolina, Tennessee, Texas, Virginia, and Wisconsin, covering the country. These gurdwaras are all members of the American Sikh Council, a national association of gurdwaras and Sikh institutions.

The surveys were directed to the adult committee or trustee members of the respective gurdwaras. I requested that the surveys be forwarded to the parents within each gurdwara through their internal email networks. Additionally, I sent out many emails using my personal family contacts across the nation. I then followed up with persistent phone calls.

Some adults were very conscientious and made it their mission to have children diligently fill the survey, while others were lax due to reasons unknown. Some children became very emotional and poured their hearts out while filling the surveys. Each bullying story from the child was unique and heart wrenching. I did run into a couple of 6th and 7th grade boys who

---

[134] 'Survey Monkey' is a survey questionnaire platform to collect data on line.

admitted to being bullied yet pleaded that I do not tell their parents and wanted to be left alone. I found it strange and hard to understand. Later, talking with my parents, I realized humans are complicated and each person's situation within their home is different, so sometimes it is difficult to help a child if they are not forthcoming and requesting help.

SURVEY RESULTS

Eventually, the survey was taken by 997 school children over a four-month period in the spring and summer of 2015. The children who took the survey were from 5–18 years old.

Approximately 86% of the children who took the survey were 11–18 years old, primarily from middle school to high school. Nearly 72% of the children were born and raised in America, while over 14% had lived in the US for 11 or more years; therefore, most were toddlers when they came to America.

718 males completed the survey and 279 were female. Over 58% of all respondents claimed to have been bullied in school. Out of those that have been bullied, nearly 60% had reported the bullying to the school authorities. The experience of bullying is very different for Sikh American boys than for the girls because the girls rarely have the distinguished marker: the turban. It is very clear that the distinguished marker of the Sikh American boys, particularly, does pose a problem based on the reactions of other kids. Sikh American boys end up bearing the brunt of the bullying, while the girls do not as they can blend in, but the boys cannot. Based on my own experience, the turban seems like a lightning rod which creates many types of emotions, mostly negative, in children. These reactions could be because of misinformation, ignorance, lack of balanced education in social studies, and media bias.

A large percentage (59%) of the Sikh American children between the ages of 5–18 responded that they were bullied. Children (see Appendix or included pie chart) ages 11–14 were bullied almost twice as much (47%) as other age groups. The next highest number (38%) of bullied children was the 15–18-year age group. To me, these are telling statistics. If the majority of the Sikh American children are bullied and stressed most of the time, how in the world are they supposed to concentrate and study?

At least 30% of the students stated that they were called out in the hallways. Over 45% of the bullying occurred in the classroom, over 31% on the bus, and nearly 30% were bullied in the restrooms. Over 17% were bullied outside school premises, while nearly 9% were bullied over the Internet.

Exactly one third of all bullied children stated that they were excluded from participating in sport activities because of the turban for the boys and due to the long hair for the girls. Nearly 9% stopped caring about why they were excluded from the team sport activities and had given up trying to participate. That is a sad situation indeed.

Of those who did get bullied, over 58% felt they were bullied because of the turban/patka/keski and nearly 29% felt they got bullied because of their hair. There is an overlap of the long, uncut hair and the turban because all turbaned Sikh American children do have uncut hair, but there are girls with uncut hair who do not wear turbans, so the range of bullied children due to the turban and/or long hair or a combination of both ranged from 58% to 87%. These numbers are cause for alarm.

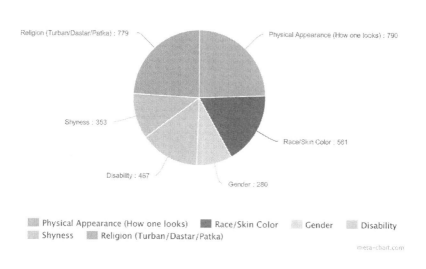

15. Why do you think students get bullied?(Check all that apply).

Children who were bullied responded overwhelmingly to questions about race, color, physical looks, and the turban. Over 56% Sikh American children thought they were being bullied because of their color/race, over 78% thought bullying was due to the turban, and over 79% thought it was due to their overall appearance.

Over 50% of all bullied respondents stated that they felt discriminated by teachers or staff in varying degrees. If the educators themselves are biased and do not treat Sikh American children with respect and sensitivity, then how can anyone expect better behavior from school children who bully others? These numbers are in contrast to my experience. Most teachers have been kind, inspiring, and respectful in order to educate students like me.

Over 26% of children were extremely motivated to confront bullies, while over 35% were quite motivated to take on bullies. An even 14% of children were somewhat motivated, while a little over 12% were only slightly motivated and over 12% were not motivated or afraid of bullies, unable to confront them. Over 38% of the children were confidant to stand up and confront bullies. Confronting bullies is one of the biggest challenges faced by children in general, and I will cover this issue in the following chapters.

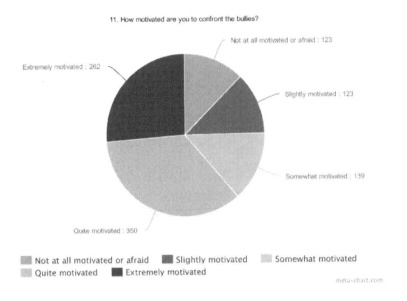

11. How motivated are you to confront the bullies?

Not at all motivated or afraid : 123

Extremely motivated : 262

Slightly motivated : 123

Somewhat motivated : 139

Quite motivated : 350

▨ Not at all motivated or afraid   ▨ Slightly motivated   ▨ Somewhat motivated
▨ Quite motivated   ▨ Extremely motivated

meta-chart.com

In order to gain overall confidence and protect themselves, children were asked if they took up any kind of martial art. A little over 23% took up some kind of martial arts and did it regularly. About 18% took up marital arts and stopped. Nearly 59% have never taken up any kind of martial arts at all.

To understand children's confidence in order to minimize shyness, one of the questions I asked was whether children participated in any kind of public speaking. Over 30% did some sort of public speaking in and/or out of school, which helped them in facing bullies. Over 28% only took up public speaking sometimes, which shows that this was not done with any passion or enthusiasm. More than three quarters of the 41% never tried public speaking, and the balance tried it and stopped.

If nearly 59% are bullied, then it seems like the rest are less likely to be bullied because they are involved in marital arts and public speaking. This indicates that children who are regularly involved in martial arts and public speaking are able to avoid bullying because of all the positive attributes of those skills (see Appendix A).

SUMMARIZED SUGGESTIONS FROM THE SURVEY

The responses from my bullying survey seem to support the bullying experienced by others and me in earlier surveys.

All the respondents taking my survey were asked for possible solutions to diminish bullying of Sikh American children. The most important suggestion, at nearly 58%, was that the children wanted "the school administration to teach Sikh history, Sikh religion and Sikh culture to the entire school" so that all the ignorance and misinformation would diminish and all school children would become informed, creating a better school environment for everyone. In addition, 39% of students suggested punishing the bullies and more empathy toward Sikh American children by the school administration as possible solutions to bullying.

The final question on the survey asked the students what would be their suggestions to improve the bullying situation. Not everyone wrote in the formal comment section, but I did receive hundreds of suggestions in a section for additional comments. The majority of suggestions fell into three major themes:

- education,
- teacher training, and
- anti-bullying classes.

> **Education:** Sikh American faith, Sikh American history, Sikh American immigration, and other experiences are scarcely mentioned in school textbooks across the nation, from elementary school to high school. Therefore, it becomes a challenge for any non-Sikh student to learn and understand about the Sikhs. Having accurate content about the Sikhs in the school curriculum so that it can be taught by the teachers and discussed in a classroom setting was the most important suggestion(s) given by all the children to reduce bullying.

Teacher training: Second, the children suggested that teachers must take more diversity training, which includes content on the Sikh Americans in order for them to understand and have some degree of empathy when dealing with the bullying, especially due to the distinguished turban. There were suggestions to hire more teachers of the Sikh faith so that there is better representation and understanding, which increases teacher diversity.

Anti-bullying classes: Third, all children need to take anti-bullying classes, but those who bully need special attention. Many suggested strong action must be taken against bullies who verbally abuse their victims in addition to taking action against physical bullying.

CONCLUSION

The results of my survey seem to be consistent with the survey done by the Sikh Coalition in 2007, which indicated that "77.5 percent of Sikh boys we surveyed who go to school in the borough of Queens report being teased or harassed on account of their Sikh identity."[135] It seems there has been no change between 2007 through 2015 in the level of bullying against turban-wearing Sikh American students. In fact, there is a slight increase across the country. All the education by Sikh American organizations for positive change to reduce bullying seems to have been jeopardized by the relentless media portrayal of negatively bearded–turban images.

Since religious identity is an intrinsic part of the Sikh faith, many Sikh American children are torn between their faith and the pull to blend in with the wider majority because of the intense peer pressure of bullying. Sometimes the bullying stops if a child has cut his/her hair to blend in.

---

[135] Hatred in the Hallways: Preliminary Report on Bias Against Sikh Students in New York City's Public Schools by Sikh Coalition

However, bullying never goes away as many times the child is considered a weakling by the bullies for giving up on their faith so easily.

The children—my peers—have poured their hearts out and given hundreds of suggestions so that bullying can be resolved. I have a sampling of the most common recommendations listed above. The statistics I have compiled here are an eye-opener, and I hope everyone who is concerned about our children's future are taking note and hopefully doing something about it.

Including Sikhs in the American curriculum is starting to happen. The states of California, New Jersey, and Texas, leaders in textbook adoption, are making changes in textbooks to include Sikhs. Currently, there is a law that has been passed in California to include material on the Sikhs in school textbooks. I am very hopeful that in the next year or so, all three states will include and adopt similar changes in their content so that all school children will start to learn about the Sikhs.

PSYCHOLOGICAL TRAUMA: INTERVIEWS WITH MENTAL-HEALTH PROFESSIONALS

"PTSD is a whole-body tragedy, an integral human event
of enormous proportions with massive repercussions."
Susan Pease Banitt[136]

Bullying is directly linked to all kinds of mental health, substance abuse, and suicide issues.

KIDS WHO ARE BULLIED

Kids who are bullied can experience negative physical, school, and mental health issues. Kids who are bullied are more likely to experience depression, anxiety, increased feelings of sadness, loneliness, changes in sleep and eating patterns, and loss of interest in activities they used to enjoy. These issues may persist into adulthood. Health complaints, decreased academic achievement in GPA, lower standardized test scores, and school participation. They are more likely to miss, skip, or drop out of school. A very small number of bullied children retaliate through extremely violent measures. In 12 out of 15 school shooting cases in the 1990s, the shooters had a history of being bullied.

---

[136] http://www.goodreads.com/quotes/tag/trauma

KIDS WHO BULLY OTHERS

Kids who bully others can also engage in violent and other risky behaviors into adulthood. Kids who bully are more likely to indulge in abuse of alcohol, other drugs in adolescence and later as adults, engage in early sexual activity, get into fights, vandalize property, and drop out of school. They can have criminal convictions and traffic citations as adults. Abusive behavior toward their partners, spouses, and adult children can also occur.

BYSTANDERS

Children who witness bullying are more likely to have increased use of tobacco, alcohol, or other drugs. There is a possibility that they have increased mental health problems, including depression, anxiety, and miss or skip school. It is a slow process, but it seems like there is a change and more bystanders are stepping up to help stop bullying, at least in my limited experience.

THE RELATIONSHIP BETWEEN BULLYING AND SUICIDE

Media reports often link bullying with suicide. However, most youth who are bullied do not have thoughts of suicide or engage in suicidal behaviors.

Although kids who are bullied are at risk of suicide, bullying alone is not the cause. Many issues contribute to suicide risk, including depression, problems at home, and trauma history. Additionally, specific groups have an increased risk of suicide, including American Indian and Alaskan Native, Asian American, lesbian, gay, bisexual, and transgender youth. This risk can be increased further when these kids are not supported by parents, peers, and schools. Bullying can make an unsupportive situation worse.[137]

---

[137] http://www.stopbullying.gov/at-risk/effects/

HIGH-RISK GROUPS BECAUSE OF BULLYING

Anyone can be bullied, but one of the highest risk groups today are the Sikh Americans. The Sikh Americans are identified as such by the federal government website www.stopbullying.gov:

> Very little research has explored bullying based on religious differences. Bullying in these situations may have less to do with a person's beliefs and more to do with misinformation or negative perceptions about how someone expresses that belief.
>
> For example, Muslim girls who wear hijabs (head scarves), Sikh boys who wear patka or dastaar (turbans), and Jewish boys who wear yarmulkes report being targeted because of these visible symbols of their religions. These items are sometimes used as tools to bully Muslim, Sikh, and Jewish youth when they are forcefully removed by others. Several reports also indicate a rise in anti-Muslim and anti-Sikh bullying over the past decade that may have roots in a perceived association of their religious heritage and terrorism.
>
> When bullying based on religion is severe, pervasive, or persistent, the Department of Justice's Civil Rights Division may be able to intervene under Title IV of the Civil Rights Act.
>
> Often religious harassment is not based on the religion itself but on shared ethnic characteristics. When harassment is based on shared ethnic characteristics, the Department of Education's Office for Civil Rights may be able to intervene under Title VI of the Civil Rights Act.[138]

There is ample data available to support this above statement. It is worrisome that if a child is continually bullied, the repressed anger may explode in many ways. The last thing anyone wants is a

---

[138] http://www.stopbullying.gov/at-risk/groups/index.html

violent repercussion. Therefore, there is a dire need to find proactive solutions.[139]

A March 13, 2014, report aired by Al Jazeera reiterated the alarming statistics: "a new survey finds two-thirds of Sikh children wearing a turban are bullied, often called 'bin Laden.'"[140] The cofounder of Sikh Coalition, Amardeep Singh, a Sikh advocacy organization formed in the aftermath of 9/11 by attorneys in 2001, stated, "The majority of Sikh children from the coasts to the heartland say that bias-based bullying is a part of their experience in school," Singh said in a press release. "We need the help of educators, administrators, lawmakers, agency officials, the media, parents, and children if we are going to end this troubling dynamic." A continuing deterioration of the environment for Sikh children will only make "trauma" a permanent facet for all turbaned Sikh children. The short and long-term repercussions absolutely do not bode well for the hundreds of thousands families and the country itself.

In the US, as a result of bullying, there are 4,400 suicides a year based on the Center for Disease Control (CDC).[141] According to National Voices for Equality Education and Empowerment (NVEEE), "100,000 students carry a gun to school each day. 28% of youths who carry weapons have witnessed violence at home. More youth violence occurs on school grounds as opposed to on the way to school.1/3 of students surveyed said they heard another student threaten to kill someone."[142]

For example, a soldier goes to war. They have to kill other humans and see the horrors of war and death continually, which causes trauma. Today, hundreds of thousands of soldiers are living with post-traumatic stress

---

[139] http://www.angriesout.com/schoolviolence/pg18.htm

[140] http://america.aljazeera.com/articles/2014/3/13/agohometerroristasikhchildrenbul-liedtwicenationalaverage.html

[141] http://nobullying.com/bullying-suicide-statistics/

[142] http://www.nveee.org/statistics/

disorder (PTSD).[143] When children go through severe bullying, they have similar experiences.

BULLYING STATISTICS

Every 7 minutes, a child is bullied. Adult intervention=4%. Peer intervention=11%. No intervention=85%.

1. Biracial and multiracial youth are more likely to be victimized than youth who identify with a single race.
2. Bullied students tend to grow up more socially anxious, with less self-esteem, and require more mental health services throughout life.
3. Only 7% of US parents are worried about cyberbullying, yet 33% of teenagers have been victims of cyberbullying
4. Kids who are obese, gay, or have disabilities are up to 63% more likely to be bullied than other children.
5. 1 million children were harassed, threatened, or subjected to other forms of cyberbullying on Facebook during the past year.
6. 86% of students said "other kids picking on them, making fun of them, or bullying them" causes teenagers to turn to lethal violence in schools.
7. It is estimated that 160,000 children miss school every day due to fear of attack or intimidation by other students.[144]
8. American schools harbor approximately 2.1 million bullies and 2.7 million of their victims.[145]
9. According to bullying statistics, 1 out of every 10 students who drops out of school does so because of repeated bullying.
10. 1 in 7 students in grades K–12 is either a bully or a victim of bullying.
11. 56% of students have personally witnessed some type of bullying at school.
12. 15% of all school absenteeism is directly related to fears of being bullied at school.

---

[143] http://www.rcpsych.ac.uk/healthadvice/problemsdisorders/posttraumaticstressdisorder.aspx

[144] National Education Association

[145] Dan Olweus, National School Safety Center

13. 71% of students report incidents of bullying as a problem at their school.

14. 90% of 4th through 8th graders report being victims of bullying.

15. Bullying statistics say revenge is the strongest motivation for school shootings. 87% of students said shootings are motivated by a desire to "get back at those who have hurt them." 86% of students said "other kids picking on them, making fun of them, or bullying them" causes teenagers to turn to lethal violence in the schools.

16. Harassment and bullying have been linked to 75% of school shooting incidents.

17. According to bullying statistics, 1 out of every 10 students who drops out of school does so because of repeated bullying.

REAL LIFE EXAMPLES OF BULLYING

There was a Sikh American kid[146] three years my senior who went through the exact same school system from kindergarten through twelfth grade as I did. This kid, Harneel, did some of the same common activities which every school kid does, including playing recreational soccer, baseball, basketball outside school but with schoolmates. He also lived in the same town and a child of two professionals. The following was his experience of bullying firsthand in his own words:

> Being alone that you are the only individual it takes a toll on you. I have been bullied countless times. It started in my third grade class where the teacher would join in with the students and make fun of me. It all started off with that I have a mouse, or a cone or a ball on my head. Couple of years ago I played recreational soccer. The opposing coach would, instead of saying Neel or No 9, would say guard the cone-head. I remember I would cry and say I did not want to go to school . . . I was the only Sikh in a body of 1640 students. Being the only Sikh in

---

[146] Harneel Singh Saini, Eastern High School, Voorhees, NJ

a turban or a patka the people did not have the awareness and
that led to the name calling and derogatory comments.[147]

This is a perfect example of how a Sikh kid is bullied off and on but
continuously throughout his childhood, from elementary to high school.
My father was personally acquainted with this family since we lived in the
same town and met on the soccer field often, the gurdwara, or would run
into them locally. This kid's grandmother was a very sensitive person who
requested my father to help when her grandson was in the 9th grade as
he was being bullied in high school.[148] My father immediately requested
time from the superintendent of the school district and made a detailed
presentation on the Sikh faith. Finally, he gave a presentation in front of
the entire school board, and the teachers which did make a positive impact
on ratcheting down the level of bullying. My father had done presentations
earlier for the entire elementary school and then the entire middle school.

Harneel was a good kid, hardworking, unassuming, shy, and nice. I have
known him since his younger brother was in the same grade as me.[149] The
bullying stress of what Harneel has stated in his YouTube video interview
is honest and matter-of-fact based on his experience. This is a very common
and disturbing theme shared by the vast majority of the Sikh American
boys across the nation.

When a child from the age of five entering kindergarten all the way
to high school—a period of thirteen years—is bullied, taunted, and traumatized, the scars are lifelong. I have never understood why nonphysical
violence does not get anyone in trouble with the law very easily, yet if the
victim retaliates to incessant bullying, he or she is suspended and/or hauled
to jail. Sustained bullying from all the research I have done can and does
often lead to PTSD. Based on current statistics, Sikh American children

---

[147] https://www.youtube.com/watch?v=WToncGLRVEM Harneel Singh's Bullying
YouTube video April 24, 2012

[148] In the year 2009

[149] http://www.gannon.edu/SpotlightDetail.aspx?id=2019 Graduated from Eastern
High School in 2011.

are being bullied at twice the national average; one can only imagine the long-term consequences on their mental and emotional well-being.[150] If these same children did not have to go through this social cruelty, there would be a much healthier and dynamic citizenry as adults rather than the reverse.[151]

On March 1, 2015, a fifth grader, Harsukh Singh, from Chattahoochee Elementary School in Duluth, Georgia, filmed himself being bullied by his schoolmates on the bus. The video went viral, with over half a million views.[152] This brave kid tried his best to counter the racial epithets—including a girl calling him a terrorist repeatedly—by his "white" schoolmates, even though he did use some profanity.[153]

Many reacted to this incident, which had gone viral on social media. One among them was Aasees Kaur, whose brother had gone through a similar harrowing experience.

Here is what Aasees Kaur has to say about the above incident in her blog on March 6, 2015:

> The viral video of a Sikh boy being called a "terrorist" on a Gwinnett County school bus should be another wake-up call to school officials in Atlanta and across the nation. Bullying remains a serious problem, but it remains to be seen whether it will receive a serious response from parents, teachers, and school officials.
>
> As a Sikh American, this issue is personal to me. Like the boy in the video, my younger brother wears a turban. For devout Sikhs, the turban is a declaration of Sikh identity, representing a commitment to the Sikh religious ideals of

---

150 http://mic.com/articles/85315/over-50-of-sikh-children-are-bullied-in-school-simply-because-of-their-faith

151 https://www.psychologytoday.com/blog/somatic-psychology/201103/child-bullying s-consequence-adult-ptsd

152 http://www.bbc.com/news/blogs-trending-31695234

153 http://www.inquisitr.com/1887447/sikh-boy-bullied-by-racist-schoolmates/

equality, justice, and love. For many, the turban reminds them of otherness, making it an easy target for mockery and even violence.

Bullying has taken a toll on my family. My brother was verbally abused in classrooms, in cafeterias during recess—and, yes, even on school buses. He was called "Osama" and "terrorist" and told to "go back to your country."

His country is this country, which we're all proud to call home. He also endured physical assaults—a broken nose and swollen jaw requiring two surgeries. In one incident, a student assaulted my brother's identity by cutting his hair, which devout Sikhs are required to keep uncut.

My brother and the boy in the video are not alone. According to Sikh Coalition surveys, a majority of Sikh students are bullied and harassed in our nation's schools—up to 67 percent in some cities. But it is not just my community. Students nationwide are being bullied because of their race, religion, nationality, gender, body type, disability, and sexual orientation.

It is important for adults to remember that bullying takes many forms. When students intentionally exclude victims from school activities and leave them socially isolated, this is bullying.

When students leave the school campus and target victims on school buses, this is bullying. The school bus is often a torment zone, where schools should be responsible for the safety of their students, but often instead turn the other way and chalk it up to "troublemaking."

When students use social media and mobile apps to target victims, this is bullying. Indeed, "cyber bullying" is uniquely problematic because it leaves victims vulnerable to slander while bullies remain anonymous.

So where do we go from here?

Parents also need to do their part, by acting like responsible adults. I have a hard time believing 12-year-olds spontaneously call each other "Osama" and "faggot" and tell people like my brother to "go back to your country" without parental influence. I shudder to think what kind of conversations these bullies' parents are having at home about people who do not look or live like them.

Above all, we need to be proactive. We have to be willing to adjust our schools' anti-bullying rules if they are not working. Just last year, in response to a federal investigation into my brother's bullying complaints, the DeKalb County School District adopted new model policies and procedures to protect students from bullying. This was a critical first step, and school districts throughout Georgia—and around the nation—should take a look at these model policies and work to plug any gaps.

I will never forget what my brother went through, and my heart aches for the child in the video, but the fight against bullying does not end when this issue fades from the headlines. Let's work together to ensure that all of our children are safe and enjoy the only childhood they will ever have."[154]

Another serious case of bullying happened a few years ago when a high school sophomore's turban was set on fire by another student, who was "white," at East Windsor High School in Hightstown, New Jersey, in 2008. Here is a report on the incident:

A routine fire drill at Hightstown High School in Mercer County turned terrifying for one student.

---

[154] http://getschooled.blog.ajc.com/2015/03/06/viral-video-of-terrorist-taunts-on-gwinnett-school-bus-points-to-larger-problems/

As students gathered outside on school grounds one morning last week, someone came up behind a 16-year-old junior, a member of the Sikh faith, and allegedly set the boy's turban on fire.

His hair was singed in several places, but he was otherwise unhurt, according to his uncle, Harjot Pannu.

"He felt like a bee stung him, and he patted on it," said Pannu. "Next thing he knew, a teacher came over and told him he was on fire."

An 18-year-old Hightstown senior, Garrett Green, was arrested hours later and charged with arson and criminal mischief, said Ben Miller, an investigator with the Hightstown Police Department.

"I was very angry and very upset and very mad initially, I could not even think straight," said the victim's mother, Sukjhot Kaur, who asked that her son's name not be printed. "The fact that something like this could have happened is beyond comprehension, especially in this day and age with the diversity we have and the way we are taught. . . . There should never be any fear of violence."[155]

My father, incidentally, knew the family and was aware of this particular incident as he was trying to help while it got quite a bit of local media attention. Initially, the police did not want to term it as a hate crime. It did require pressure from the community, activist attorneys, and the American Sikh Council to get the police to pursue more serious charges. Somehow, minorities seem to require extra pressure in order for the authorities to do the right thing. There is some institutional bias which, hopefully, is changing for the better day by day.

Having to deal with this is "normal" for most children of the Sikh faith, and they have to bear this on an almost daily basis. There is yet to be an

---

[155] http://immigrationvoice.org/forum/archive/index.php/t-19095.html

in-depth study on the mental trauma on Sikh children due to long-term bullying. It will be helpful to see a detailed report so lawmakers and society become aware of this insidious and despicable behavior by children who bully others.

INTERVIEWS WITH CHILD PSYCHIATRISTS AND CHILD PSYCHOLOGISTS

The reason I wanted to reach out to mental-health professionals was to find out the effects of bullying on children's emotional health. I was able to speak with seven child psychiatrists and psychologists from across the East Coast who were kind enough to spare their valuable time in order for me to get my interviews completed. I also wanted to confirm my fears that bullying was severe enough to warrant all the effort by millions of parents and adults trying to dissipate this destructive evil which haunts school systems throughout the country. I contacted over thirty five child psychiatrists, child psychologists, and child counselors.

By talking to all these experts, I came to realize that there are solutions, some simple, others complicated, but most require a change in the mental conditioning of all those involved through education in world religions, history, and culture, at a minimum. This education is not something to be given in one little dose in 6th grade but should be given in continuous doses starting from 1st grade onward so that by the time a child goes to middle school, they are mentally prepared to accept anyone and everyone without any hesitation.

Further, the system has to change for the better with novel, out-of-the-box ideas to deal with an ever-changing landscape within classrooms, especially with the increase in non–European Americans in last few decades. Catering to the newer Americans is as important as the not-so-new Americans because no can be left behind.

A bullied child, if scarred for life, is a handicapped citizen, in a way, and cannot develop his/her full potential as an adult to be the most productive citizen they can be. America needs every able-bodied person to give their best. This can only happen if every child studies in a bully-free environment so that they turn out to be bright, talented, and emotionally happy human beings.

The seven personal interviews I conducted with child psychiatrists and psychologists were based on a set of questions (see Appendix B). I asked the questions via telephone. The verbal responses were written down by me. I designed a set of questions primarily focusing on the possible solutions for bullying and its negative long-term effects.

On the "effects of bullying on 6–15 years of age," most of the experts agreed that bullying does affect the children's self-esteem, causing depression and isolation. According to Dr. Surinder Singh Sodhi, "They (bullies) are satisfying their need of power, have a mental illness, and in the process the weaker child gets punished. Since Sikh kids wear turbans they are made easy targets. One way of stopping bullying is to stand up to them—in this case the bully."[156] The suggested solutions of the professionals varied based on the level of severity of the bullying, and most agreed that school performance is negatively impacted.

I can still remember the last day of school in 7th grade. It was a bright and beautiful day. Since I walked to middle school normally, I got to meet people on my way. That particular day, I had just reached the entrance of the school parking lot when a school bus passed by and I heard a girl yell out, "Osama-raghead," repeating it a few times while laughing. I was shocked and taken aback. I continued walking toward the school building entrance while the school bus stopped to drop off the kids. As luck would have it, a school teacher was parking her car when this incident happened. She immediately took action by approaching the school bus and demanding that the perpetrator own up to the bullying incident or else everyone would get suspended. Very quickly, an 8th grade African American girl confessed to the incident. She was suspended for a day and was made to offer me a written apology. I was just fortunate that a good teacher took swift action; otherwise, it would bother me for a long time, especially when it was a faceless voice from a bus trying to bully me.

---

[156] My personal interviews with child psychiatrists and child psychologists

Since I was raised and trained to handle some of these issues, I normally do not get angry or react immediately. Most children at that age will react in ways which are impulsive and, more than likely, violent. Insulting someone's faith or mother and/or loved one can get you into serious trouble. Children need to be taught by their parents and teachers to be respectful in these matters. Fallout from this kind of bullying can become violent because this touches on personal insults. In most cultures, family and religious honor is paramount, and even kids can be very sensitive to these transgressions. The feedback from the mental-health professionals reassured me that my parents did teach me all the right skills to handle such situations. I have been fortunate in having good friends, gaining self-confidence over time, learnt more about my faith, trained to be tolerant, to always challenge oppression, have a healthy dose of self-esteem, and it so happens that these ideas have been suggested by all the psychiatrists I had interviewed.

Since childhood bullying over a long period does leave a lasting scar, I was curious how does one diagnose it? The professionals I spoke to described bullied victims tend to develop behaviors of anxiety. Bullied victims tend to experience depression more than their peers who have not been involved in bullying, which can lead to academic problems, frequent absences from school, loneliness, and social isolation. According to the experts' experience, victims are also at risk for having attention deficit hyperactivity disorder (ADHD).

Bullied children have been found to have increased risks of suicidal thoughts and actions in both boys and girls. However, research indicates that the risk of both thoughts and attempts at suicide seem to be higher for girl victims, regardless of repeated bullying. In the case of boys, the risk of suicidal thoughts seems to increase in bullied victims when the bullying occurs repeatedly.

In cases of serious bullying, the child can be diagnosed with post-traumatic stress disorder (PTSD). Studies have shown there is no definitive method to prove or disprove whether a child does have PTSD, which typically is associated with adult veteran of wars. Nevertheless, the professionals I interviewed were of the opinion that emotional abuse causing severe trauma can be equated to PTSD as some of the symptoms are issues such as anxiety, depression, and flashbacks.

In order to treat PTSD, many of the professionals suggested that the bullied victim and the parents must seek help from counselors and psychologists. The child should not take medications; instead, the trauma should be healed with psychotherapy. Parents, teachers, and friends should be supportive, and the child must be placed in a social setting slowly so that interaction with others heals the emotional wounds. By reliving the experience, over time this can be treated through counseling.

For Sikh American children, in particular, who have gone through harrowing experiences, such as the bully forcibly cutting a child's hair, the bully lighting a child's turban on fire, or the bully removing a child's turban and beating them senseless, are the real life cases which I discussed during my interviews. Some of the ideas suggested were in the following order of importance: to inform the school authorities, the police, the media, and, finally, the legislators. As Dr. Kanwar Sidhu stated, "A firm stand must be taken to deal with this by the parents."[157] Additionally, the professional did stress that the parents should help instill more confidence and give plenty of support to their child and never make the child feel guilty for any reason. In discussion with my parents and other adults, I believe serious bullying situations such as these must be highlighted carefully in the media so that the public understands the issue.

When a child in elementary and/or middle school is ostracized or shunned by a teacher, the consequences can be demoralizing for the student. A child can be confused, not knowing whom to go to, because normally children look up to teachers to solve problems and not the ones creating them. Dr. Massi Shamilov emphatically stated, "The child must let the parents know and the parents must talk to the teacher or administration as that kind of behavior cannot be tolerated."[158] The professionals I spoke

---

[157] My personal interviews with child psychiatrists and child psychologists
[158] Ibid

to seem to agree that the parents must have an open communication with their own child so that he/she can discuss any issues, such as bullying by a teacher. Further, schools should take the initiative so that teachers acquire diversity training.

One of the questions I had modeled was how would empathy training help in reducing bullying? Most of the professionals agreed that "empathy training" would be important and a hallmark of the overall education in schools, which could include existing informational content produced by Sikh American organizations. A few of the professionals did not see too much value in this kind of training to be made mandatory. One professional also advocated that the only solution was to challenge the oppressor.

While discussing solutions for Sikh American children who wear religiously mandated headgear, such as turbans, the professionals came up with very practical suggestions, many of which I continue to use in my own life. The consensus of suggestions revolved around having the child be more informed about their own faith, being able to educate their friends and schoolmates, and increase the level of interaction with everyone, including the local community, in order to dispel ignorance.

Following up on the previous question, I had queried the professionals about how could the school administration help in improving the current situation of bullying. There were a wide spectrum of answers and all were sound in their analysis. Schools must take responsibility for the actions of bullies and enforce consequences. As Dr. Pal Singh Brar put it, "The school administration needs to reprimand the bullies, have them expelled from school. The school should educate others about the Sikh religion."[159] Empathy training should be a hallmark of education. Teachers should identify the problem and solve with a constructive solution.

The administrations should seriously consider inviting representatives from any of the Sikh American advocacy organizations to give talks in order to educate the school community. I know for a fact that in many

---

[159] My personal interviews with child psychiatrists and child psychologists

states, but especially in the state of New Jersey, learning about the Jewish Holocaust is mandatory by law as I went through this class. Once a year, representatives from Jewish advocacy organizations go to every middle school in the state and teach about the Holocaust. The same exact setup can be done at the minimum for teaching the children in schools about Sikh Americans.

Most bullying from my personal experience and my research shows that bullying occurs away from the gaze of adults. When I asked the professionals what could be done to fend off those bullies who bully in the shadows, There were an array of suggestions. A few suggested to avoid being alone, leave the place as safety was important, speak up, and try to become more confidant, including informing the school authorities. Self-confidence and self-empowerment were some of the other strong suggestions. Dr. Akashdeep Ajula indicated that "The bullied child should be aware of his rights, informed about hate crimes, and should bring it to the attention of authorities."[160]

CONCLUSION

The interviews I did with the mental-health professionals were enlightening. I hope this data helps in raising awareness among all the administrators, legislators, and the general public across the country to take action by a "call to arms" in order to stop bullying in its tracks—today and not tomorrow—otherwise, we might lose another innocent child to bullying.

It was pretty clear that bullying does negatively impact the mental health of the bullied victim in several ways. Based on the survey I have conducted in the previous chapter, it is distressing to see the unnecessary stress and trauma Sikh American children have to deal with in daily life. Instead of concentrating on their studies and other extracurricular activities, which would make them dynamic and happy citizens, Sikh American children are saddled with this extra burden of bullying.

---

[160] Ibid

Even though some of the ideas and suggestions given here are basic common sense, it helps when professionals give direction and input. Suggestions from professionals are taken more seriously by educators than from lay parents in order to solve an issue like bullying earnestly.

STRATEGIES FOR FAMILIES

"Everyone thinks of changing the world,
but no one thinks of changing himself."
Leo Tolstoy[161]

WHAT KIDS CAN DO TO STOP BULLYING

Nothing stops you from being friendly. A nice smile—it is completely free! There was boy a year ahead of me in school in elementary school who happened to be a Sikh.[162] He was a big, shy, quiet, self-assuming kid with a perpetual smile plastered to his face. It is never easy even for a bully to harass someone who is polite and is smiling all the time. Not only has this kid's smile remained, but he is extremely bright, who is never involved in any school politics, which adds to his personality trait with less chances of getting bullied. As a freshman in high school, he did take a year of training in boxing from a professional trainer outside school, though. This definitely helped him in his overall self-confidence to tackle any intimidation, if any, in addition to his physique.

Get to know other kids, and let them know who you are. It does take effort and some work to be an extrovert if you are naturally shy. Therefore,

---

[161] http://www.brainyquote.com/quotes/topics/topic_change.html#50jR351M0wWAD2A8.99

[162] Lovejot Singh. My father did one of his presentations to the Elementary school on Lovejot's father's request as he was bullied while in 4th grade. The bullying did stop after my father addressed the entire school.

I have suggested several solutions in the following pages, mostly all from my own personal experiences while growing up.

Don't be selfish and don't think you are number one as people around you could be better in other things.

Make friends, be nice, and be cool!

Take a stand, hold your head high, look people in the eye. Like my father always taught us, "Think like a Tiger, act like a Tiger, look like a Tiger, walk like a Tiger, everyone will think you are a Tiger, and treat you like one."

BE INVOLVED IN PUBLIC SPEAKING

The day I turned 3 years old, my father had me on the podium in front of the congregation at our local gurdwara, saying the Sikh greeting to everyone. This started my journey in public speaking. Every year, my father organized a public speaking competition which was part of national competition called the Sikh Youth Symposium.[163] I have been competing for the last twelve years and reached the nationals twice. I made it to the regional (state) level five times. Typically, the topics have ranged from religion, history, and social issues. Not only have the topics made me learn and research more, which strengthened the foundational knowledge in my own faith and heritage, but also increased my confidence in self-worth, thereby being able to convey the knowledge to my peers in school whenever the occasion arose.

Public speaking has several benefits, but most of all, it gives the person self-confidence, which directly effects self-esteem and eliminates shyness. Talking in front of an audience is always a challenge for the vast majority the world over. Rarely does it come naturally as this is something a child has to be trained and groomed for in order to be good at it eventually. Shyness in children is the number one reason for not being able to speak up when being bullied in any shape or form. It is imperative that every child

---

[163] http://sikhyouthalliance.org/ Sikh Youth Alliance of North America (SYANA), Toledo, Ohio.

be trained to be a public speaker as it is one of the basic building blocks to overcome bullies and bullying, not to mention a valuable lifelong skill.

At a public speaking competition held in New Jersey at the age of seven in 2005

But all Sikh American youngsters need to up the game to a much higher level, like the trailblazing Serene Singh, a senior at Rampart High School in Colorado Springs, Colorado.[164] Serene, a Sikh American, became a National Forensics League (NFL) national champion in 2014.[165] Her older sister, Norene Singh, was a NFL finalist in 2012. All kids need to come out of their comfort zone and be involved in the NFL eventually in order to train and compete at the highest level. The NFL is the best speech and debate national organization made to prepare middle school and high school students in the art of public speaking. The preparation and training

---

[164] http://gazette.com/colorado-springs-student-takes-her-talents-to-the-other-nfl/article/1509047

[165] http://chsaanow.com/2014-03-25/state-speech-tournament-final-results/ Original Oratory: 1st: Serene Singh, The Classical Academy (Sorry) - National Champion

for NFL is intense and will make you a sharper and much more confident individual who can think on their feet. Winning any level of the NFL is a bonus and icing on the cake. My dad tried getting the school in my town to start the NFL through the administration and elected officials but never got any help or positive feedback. Also, there were no local schools doing it where I could join as a member, because if there were, my dad would have dragged me into it in a heartbeat. Nevertheless, whatever I have done so far has been extremely helpful.

Between my public speaking skills and passion for human rights, I was very fortunate to be invited to speak at the United Nations in Geneva, Switzerland, in March 2015 to present a paper on human rights violations that Sikhs have been facing for decades in India.[166] This was, indeed, an honor to speak at such an august gathering.

BE INVOLVED IN CUB SCOUTS OR BOY SCOUTS AND GIRL SCOUTS

My father and my grandfather were involved in Scouting during their time growing up; therefore, it became just normal that my brother and I would be continuing the tradition. My parents were both involved in the initial stages of my Cub Scouts years. Getting together with other parents and the Cubs every other week was just a fun time I looked forward to regularly. I do not recall anyone in my den during my Cub Scout years being mean or bigoted. My father was very social and friendly with every one of the parents as that was his personality, which did help break many barriers, which I now realize. Kids by and large do not see the same differences as adults do unless and until they are conditioned to do otherwise. In my case, even though there were predominantly Caucasian kids of various Christian denominations and the Jewish faith, there were also kids of other ethnicities and faiths. My father did his part in making the overall experience interesting and went out of his way to answer even the silliest questions by Cubs or their parents about the "turban" and/or our faith.

---

[166] Invited at the behest of the Sikh Educational Trust, Edmonton, Canada

My years from Tiger to Bear and then Webelo I to Webelo II were filled with fun activities, some outdoor and others indoors. But each activity was an adventure with a lot of comradery. These friendships helped build bridges at school since those kids who were in the "pack" with me had common interests which helped in diminishing any chances of bullying.

Quite few of my Cub Scout friends, even though some went to the other elementary schools within the township, all landed up at the same Boy Scout troop—Troop 48, Berlin, New Jersey. My dad took me to three other troops to check them out, but fortunately, we simply opted for the one where my friends went. That was the best decision I ever made. The troop had nearly 50 Scouts when I joined in the spring of 2009.

My first trip within a few weeks after joining Troop 48 was to Hickory Run in Northern Eastern Pennsylvania for a camping and whitewater rafting trip. We left on a Friday evening, reaching Hickory Run at 11 pm in the light rain. By the time my buddy Nick and me set up our tent, it was past midnight. Nick was a year ahead of me but the nicest kid you would ever meet. We became friends right off the bat. We slept like logs as we were so tired after struggling to put up our tent. In the morning, it was my turn to make breakfast and I had never made scrambled eggs. While I was making a mess of the eggs, I could see Mike, my Scoutmaster, gently pulling my dad aside so that I could make mistakes and learn from them without any help from my father. This was one of many life lessons learnt while camping without my father or any adult assisting. The last six and half years in Boy Scouts have been an incredible experience.

Those life skills which are taught in corporate America, such as leadership, team building, mentoring, organizing, planning, respectful opinion, solution-oriented ideas, conflict resolution, proper manners, and much more, is learnt by Scouts practically in a safe environment. I have learnt all these life skills in varying degrees, which actually gives me a leg up in overall confidence, which, in turn, minimizes bullying.

The camaraderie and friendships built within the Boy Scout troop is something hard to describe to others who have not been in Scouting. I do not recall a bad experience in all my years. Everyone, regardless of social or class background, were pretty respectful. In fact, due to my father's deep involvement with the troop and everyone in it, even those who could be possibly less friendly ended up going the extra mile by offering to comb my hair and tie our patkas on weekend and summer camping trips when my father was not there. Kids are always inquisitive about everything, so I made it a point to groom my hair and tie my patka/turban in the company of my fellow scouts, which very quickly took away any mystique or unwanted questioning. The younger adults in charge of the overall leadership within our troop definitely helped in making my time in scouting a breeze. The adult Scout leaders, like my Scoutmaster, Mike McCormick, and Assistant Scoutmasters, Mike Gallagher and Tom Ferrari, need to be specially mentioned for selflessly volunteering their time to make my life in Scouting completely worthwhile. All this further strengthened the overall experience and, thankfully, never had any bullying within scouting.

My Eagle Scout project at the Stafford Trail, Voorhees, NJ, on June 21, 2012

I was having so much fun camping that, for the first year, I did not do more than one or two merit badges. Eventually, I had to work on getting my merit badges, and with my father's constant prodding, speeded up the process of going through the ranks that I finished my Eagle Scout project in the summer of 2012 as I graduated from 8th grade. I managed to do my final board of review and finished by Eagle Award before I turned 15 in February of 2013. I was fortunate that my Uncle Ramneek, Aunt Manal, sisters, Meher and Ammer, were all there at my Eagle Court of Honor held in May 2013. It was, indeed, an achievement which not only my entire family but also my Scoutmaster Mike McCormick and other adult leaders, like Mike Gallagher, were proud of, and I was glad that I was able to achieve the Eagle Award through this team effort.

A MEMORABLE BACKPACKING TRIP

I planned a trip with my backpacking crew to the Grand Tetons in 2011—a year in advance of our actual trip. We and a total of six boys who eventually went for the trip with three adults, including my Scoutmaster, Mike, Assistant Scoutmaster, Tom and my good friend Don's dad, Dr. Massi Shamilov. My father has always shown leadership by leading and doing things first so others can emulate the same. So, I raked leaves, mowed lawns, shoveled snow, and did odd errands for friends and neighbors 'til I collected over half of the money required to go for the trip. My parents put in the rest.

Finally, in August 2012, the our backpacking crew embarked on its most ambitious trip to date—an 11 day trip to Wyoming, including four days in Yellowstone National Park and six days backpacking in Grand Teton National Park at an elevation of over 11,000 feet above sea level.

After we visited the amazing Yellowstone Park, we finally started on our backpacking trip. Not everyone in our crew was acclimatized to the high elevation we planned to climb. Nevertheless, right on our first day, two of our crewmates had some issues: one was having breathing problems, possibly because of the altitude, and the other had sprained his ankle. So,

Dr. Shamilov stepped up to take them both back to base camp and just do day trips for the next six days, while the rest of us carried on! The rugged mountains, the varied landscape, the serenity, the solitude, crystal clear lakes filled with wild trout, the pristine air was just overwhelmingly beautiful to take in in such a short time. It was pure intoxication! We had to carry bear cans to store our food in case of bears came prowling into our tents at night. We saw caribou, bears, eagles in this rugged landscape, living like they have always lived for thousands of years.

We finally made it to our destination at a point on the Grand Tetons at an elevation of 11,500 feet. Tired but excited, it made the overall trip unbelievably memorable, all thanks to the camaraderie within our troop.

Our backpacking crew of nine with me (4th from the right)—
Grand Tetons, Wyoming, Aug 2012

The "fab four" on top of the Grand Tetons—Don, Pranav, Luke, and me

Talk about diversity and genuinely respecting each other—all four of us who completed the backpacking trip are from the Jewish, Hindu, Christian, and Sikh faiths, but that has never mattered because only then can genuine friendship flourish.

A lot of planning, coordination, communication, teamwork, and collective leadership among my peers in my Scout troop made the trip to Wyoming a wild success.

I have done five 50-plus-mile backpacking trips in groups of 4–11 over the last few years. These are aside from the several 10–20-mile hikes on the Eastern seaboard. The love for nature, the friendships, just makes it so much more interesting to be part of Scouting.

BE A MENTOR IN SCHOOL

I volunteered to be a mentor in 8th grade, which not only forces you to be an extrovert if you are not but also makes you interact with all the kids and adults who come through the school. It teaches you communication skills, people skills, such as manners, how to talk to people, but more importantly, other kids, especially one's peers, see you doing something positive, which is not easy to negatively counter by bullies. My personal experience was certainly good as I interacted with many kids who would not have spoken to me otherwise, and in the bargain, they learnt who I was and realized that I was no different than them—just a normal human being who happens to follow a different faith.

Join and participate in school activities, such as various clubs, as there are many starting right from 6th grade in middle school. These clubs are outlets for any passion a student may have with the added advantage of making friends with like-minded peers. The more schoolmates become your friends, the less likely the chances of bullying. Remember, even make friends with the person kids rarely talk to— the janitor. We are all humans, and each and every one must be respected, especially the lowly and genuine respect will be reciprocated in more ways than you will ever know or see.

BECOME A COACH FOR SOCCER, BASKETBALL, BASEBALL, GOLF, ETC.

While going through middle school and playing intramural soccer, I actually saw high school kids who were coaching soccer teams from grades 1–8 with their own parents helping as assistants. What a way to give back to the community and also be involved with kids a few years younger, to be able lead through leadership. I did not become a soccer coach but would recommend any kid to try it as it shows several positive traits, all decreasing the chances of getting bullied. My younger brother, who is thirteen and in 8th grade, wanted to be a referee with the Voorhees Soccer Association in the spring of 2015 but could not as he had to be fourteen in order to be selected. I guess he will wait till the fall of 2015 to turn fourteen and then become a soccer referee. Being a referee puts you in the middle of all the action in the field, and kids playing get to see you as someone who is knowledgeable with authority. Being a kid of the Sikh faith gives you the advantage as being looked at positively.

JOIN THE STUDENT COUNCIL

In 9th grade, I unsuccessfully ran for student council to be the secretary. I made posters and communicated with many of my friends and peers by texting, using twitter, etc. But as anyone knows, getting elected in high school is purely a popularity contest. By 10th grade, I had made many more friends, but my socializing activities directly affected my grades. I did not stand for election to the student council, but the feedback from my peer group was that I would win a position hands down if I ran. My parents put their foot down and came down hard on my electronic media exploits. This did put a damper on my social life, but it brought my focus back on my studies to get my grades up in 11th grade. During the fourth quarter of my junior year, I ran for the president of the student council, with many kids voting for me, but for some odd reason lost to my opponent, who had been the president since freshman year. It was a real disappointment, but my parents were very positive about it. Student council puts you in the middle of the issues of leadership, team building, diplomacy, and many other skills which are not only advantageous in the long run but also allow you to be seen as mature and confident among your peers. This in itself helps reduce bullying to a large extent.

BE INVOLVED IN MARTIAL ARTS

Kids should enroll in any kind of martial arts. I was 3 years old back in March 2001, and before I even realized what I was doing, my parents put me into the MacKenzie Karate School in Voorhees. I had a neighbor and friend who was the same age who also joined at the same time. I slowly realized that the reason I stayed on to train in Taekwondo was that it gave me a sense of having an indomitable spirit, not to give in, and secondly, Taekwondo helped me learn how to defend myself.

My teacher was a wonderful young man—Master Rory, a graduate of Cherry Hill East High School, who was about 20 years old and great with little kids. I was the youngest kid at that time to join the school. My first day's Polaroid photograph looked like a little Chinese doll with a tuft on the head in a white uniform, striking a karate pose by trying to put on a mean face.

My father would diligently walk me to the school as we lived close by and later drove regularly to at least four classes a week. Master Rory left when I turned six, and I missed his friendly demeanor. Karate became second nature, and the school was a like a second home, especially 'til I got my black belt at age nine.

Master Robert Turley, a 5th *dan* in Hapkido and a 4th *dan* in Taekwondo, made it fun and hard at the same time. I noticed all the kids, young and old, actually listened and conformed to every word he spoke. He happened to be a retired supervisor from the Camden Penitentiary system. Slowly, some of the people who joined with me dropped out and didn't come anymore as time went by, but I continued because I liked the dojo and made new friends there. At my red belt graduation, I heard Master Turley say, "The red belt is a sign of danger and bravery!" I liked all the training which was taught at MacKenzie's Karate. When I first joined Taekwondo, I did not know anything. But by the time I turned eight, I had learned never to give in and to fight bullies without raising a fist. By the way, my parents' private boarding school motto was also "never give in"!

I liked when some of the senior black belts at my belt tests used to do demonstrations by jumping, fly kicking, and kicking higher than I could even imagine. I also loved watching them do their weapon demonstrations too. My favorite pattern was Choong-Moo. The reason I liked this is because it had the awesome flying side kick in it.

I broke my first board at one of my belt tests in 2004 with my bare hand and learned how to do a flying side kick to break another board in half. All my belts and many trophies that I earned over the last 14 years are displayed on my bedroom wall.

I received my poom belt in November 2006 and practiced and worked very hard on my patterns and strength training for my black belt test held on May 20, 2007. Reaching this ultimate goal had been something I had certainly looked forward to for a long time.

The MacKenzie's school student creed stated:

- I intend to develop myself in a positive manner and avoid anything that would reduce my mental growth or physical health.
- I intend to develop my self-discipline in order to bring out the best in myself and in others.
- I intend to use what I have learned in class both constructively and defensively to help myself and my fellowmen, and never to be abusive or offensive.

I earned my 3rd *dan* in Taekwondo in October 2012 and my 1st *dan* in Hapkido in October 2013 by the age of 15. All this training and effort paid off based on 14 years in Taekwondo and nearly 6 years in Hapkido. My parents spent a large sum of money between my brother and me, but that was the best money spent to stop bullying. My father loved calling it an "anti-bullying insurance policy." My brother and I can personally attest to the fact that all the thousands of dollars my parents spent on us actually paid off by keeping bullies at bay.

Receiving my 3rd *dan* and my brother, Sherveer,
his 2nd *dan* in Taekwondo in October 2012

I also took classes and spent two summers learning the Sikh martial arts known as "Gatka," which is a, primarily, fighting art using various weapons like the long sword, punch dagger, the chakri (a rope and wire contraption which has to be spun at speed over and around your body), a chakkar (metal Frisbee which can slice a person's head off, if needed), and the nagni (a 10 to 15 feet long, 2-inch wide metal strip whipped all around one's body). Regular training is done with long sticks instead of metal implements.

I still remember my parents being a little nervous on my first day entering middle school. As luck would have it, the first kid I ran into on the opening day's school chaos loudly proclaiming, "Aren't you the kid with the Black belt?" and I enthusiastically replied, "Yes!" My day was made—actually, my year was made. Not only did Jon Raphael become my friend, but no one dared touch me for the foreseeable future.

In 8th grade, one of my classmates was brought up by a single mother with no discipline at all. This Caucasian kid who sat next to me would find some stupid thing to say in the middle of the class period so that others could hear and get a kick out of it. He would physically poke me or hit me, and I asked him to stop a few times, but he persisted. One day, fortunately for me and unfortunately for him, when he picked on me physically, I used a martial arts move and twisted his hand. Before he knew it, his head had bounced off the desk so hard that he was in a daze while the class teacher was looking the other way. Too embarrassed to complain, he did not utter a word. Not only did he leave me alone and stop his silly bullying, but he was quiet for a week. He finally got the courage to come up to me and ask me where I learnt the karate skills. I directed him to my dojo and ended up enrolling him as a student. Not only is this kid still there, but his mother and he now talk to me respectfully whenever they see me.

PARTICIPATE IN SOME SPORT ACTIVITY IN SCHOOL

Getting involved in some team event is ideal as one progresses to know others on the team and vice versa. But there are other individual sport activities which still involve peers who get to see you in a different light if you immerse yourself with passion and not just biding time. I practiced for a few months as a sophomore on my own and then joined the track team for cross country when I became a junior. It reignited my friendships with kids I was friends in elementary school, others from cub scouts, but most of all, it helped me blossom and mature through the program. The health and fitness part was just a bonus.

I was average and my timings were not great, but now, not only do I have a lifelong passion for running but made so many friends with common interests and that bonding has helped the overall high school experience, which no child should miss because of bullying or other issues.

Doing the mile at Eastern High School
at a track meet in November 2014

OTHER CULTURAL ACTIVITIES

One of the programs I did participate was to showcase "bhangra," an extremely upbeat, energizing cultural dance from the land of Punjab. Even though "bhangra" is not directly related to the Sikh faith, it is ingrained into the people from Punjab and its culture for centuries; therefore, it has been part of the Sikhs, who have primarily spread this cool energizing dance throughout the diaspora globally. Today, there are intercollegiate "bhangra" competitions across the US, including nearly all the Ivy League universities, which are increasing the awareness indirectly about the Sikhs and their cultural heritage.

In 2013, while in 9th grade, I was able to present a 5–6 minute "bhangra" mix on stage at Eastern High School in front of hundreds of my peers. The cheers, screams, and applause was worth all the effort it took to practice and showcase as it made me feel completely normal to be bicultural and yet be an American. Due to the success, I was able to do it again in 2014, and I know it was even better the second time around because over a dozen or more girls sitting behind my parents in the third row from the front were jumping in their seats while screaming their heads off. Confidence through "coolness" does help in dissipating bullying in many unseen ways.

Be helpful, and always smile! It is free and goes a long way to disarm bullies.

Performing "bhangra," an energizing dance
at Eastern high School in April 2013

With my friends who came specially to support me
at Eastern High School in April 2014

WHAT PARENTS CAN DO TO MINIMIZE BULLYING

One cause of Sikh kids being bullied continuously is because of the lack of proactive parental support. This is not as simple as it sounds, yet it does not require loads of time. The vast majority of parents are already aware of bullying from their own personal experiences or stories heard from others and their own children. It behooves every concerned parent to plan to get involved, for example, in a small school fair or in a science exhibit or a fund raising event. Not to mention any and all parent–teacher conferences, even if your child is acing their studies. If a child's parent is a regular face in the school hallways or in local community events, other children will see you as normal as themselves and less as the "other" or foreign or a stranger. Interaction and communication is the key to breaking all kinds of stereotyping and misconceptions, even among teachers and administrators.

If all the parents put in extra effort by joining the PTA and at least trying to help, word spreads quickly through the grapevine that a parent who happened to be a Sikh American is indeed a nice person, and that changes the attitude and perception of the observing adult, who then also talks to their children, which eventually makes a positive change finally helping reduce bullying.

My mother was a "room mom" when I was in kindergarten all the way to 5th grade. Room moms primarily help and assist teachers in class, on school trips, outings, etc., and other children see an active mother who is helpful, nice, and then the perception of the children changes and they see someone like me as normal as themselves. My mother was a "room mom" for my younger brother too from 1st–4th grade! This also helped build a rapport with the teachers who may keep an eye out for someone like me in case I did get bullied. Regardless of the level of education or language skills, parental interaction is important. If it is a real challenge, then it falls on the parents to ask for help within the faith community in order to assist their child.

Since there is still no information about the Sikhs in general in any of the school textbooks across the nation, therefore, the only other way to remove ignorance is by personally educating the folks in the schools. There are plenty of resources today which include ready-made presentations for various audiences, from elementary to high school kids.[167] It is a tough and painstaking process which takes up valuable time and energy, but there is no way around it if you want your children to thrive and not simply survive. My father has done many presentations throughout my school years to all the students, teachers, and even the administrators. Having an activist father did help because everyone knew who he was; therefore, all the kids knew who we were! My father has always led by example. He tried his very best to be an exemplary model to inspire my brother and me. Finally, in September of 2014, my father was nominated to be on the Voorhees School

---

[167] Videos, You-tubes videos, power point presentation, literature, tri-fold, brochures, general information on the Sikhs all produced by well-meaning Sikh Americans from Sikh Coalition to the American Sikh Council

District Advisory Board, and we were all honored by the gesture made by the school district authorities.

My parents have made it a point to take part in as many school activities as possible because unless other parents, teachers, interact and communicate with each other, there always be perceptions of others—both negative and positive. The whole point here is to minimize the negative, if any, through positive proactive action so that the people who make up the schools see you through a healthier lens.

HAVE A PARENT BECOME A COACH

My father made it his mission to proactively interact with the local community. In 4th grade, I joined the intramural soccer in Voorhees, and my father immediately signed up to become a soccer coach. Fall soccer is played for over ten weeks, and my father and his good friend Mike both started coaching as Coach Mike's twin sons, Andrew and Colin, were also my good friends and on the same team. The minimum spent was two days of practice of an hour and half each time every week, plus the weekend tournament. It took away three evenings and at least 6 hours of time each week to organize and run the team. My father did this for eight solid years—five of them with me and three with my younger brother.

There are approximately 1,100 kids participating in soccer year-round in our town. Over a thousand kids, their parents, relatives, and friends all end up seeing not only someone like my brother and me on the soccer field but my father being a coach just like anyone else. Over the years, while accompanying my father in a shopping mall or the grocery store, random kids have come up and said, "Hi, Coach," to my father, and I can see the knowing smile on his face. That is tremendous positive exposure without opening your mouth except by simply mentoring others. If more fathers and mothers became active and simply started to coach, it would make a great impact by giving back to the local community and in minimizing bullying.

My father coaching his team, the "Toronto FC,"
with my brother in September 2014

If soccer was not enough, my father became an assistant Scoutmaster in my Boy Scout troop in early 2010. Most troops and ours is no different; typically, the active parents and adult leaders, like my father, would carpool and take the scouts on the monthly weekend camping trips. My father made most of the trips 'til my brother made Eagle in August 2014 and then slowed down on the trips as he was so busy doing much more within Scouting at the national level.[168]

PARTICIPATE IN INTERFAITH COUNCILS

Parents should get involved in the local interfaith councils. Again, unless and until parents interact and educate other adults about their faith and heritage,

---

[168] My brother, Sherveer, is one of the youngest Eagle Scouts in the nation as he finished at the age of 12 years and 10 months. He should be finishing his Hornaday Badge Award by the end of 2015. My father just completed his Wood Badge in record time of 26 days, got approved by BSA, and got his "beads" on October 7, 2015.

others sometimes will not make an effort to learn on their own. My father has been involved with the Interfaith Center of Greater Philadelphia (ICGP) since its inception in 2004 off and on.[169] Even though there are two gurdwaras in the Philadelphia area—one in Millbourne and another in Upper Darby—there has been very little interaction from the Sikhs. Aside from my father and another active lady, Ashvinder Kaur Metha, who have worked with the ICGP on furthering interfaith understanding, there has been literally no one educating them about the Sikh faith. These are all building blocks of human understanding, and many are needed to create harmony everywhere.

My brother, my parents, and I have participated in several "Interfaith Peace Walks" which have been held in conjunction with the ICGP in Philadelphia over the years. The Sikh American participation from the local gurdwaras in these walks were led by Yashpal Singh Bains, his wife, Manjit Kaur Bains, and their daughter, Dr. Upneet Kaur Bains, for many years, which they still continue.

My brother and me attending the Interfaith
Peace Walk in Philadelphia, April 2013

---

[169] http://www.interfaithcenterpa.org/#!history/c1osm

PARTICIPATE IN VARIOUS PARADES

My father, with the help of other adults within the community, did organize the local Sikhs to participate in July 4th parade in Philadelphia on more than one occasion. I remember, in 2006, standing on a float with my family, dressed in red, white, and blue while waving to the crowds on a beautiful day in downtown Philadelphia. I had the privilege to participate in many Memorial Day parades locally in my own town, dressed in my scout uniform, especially when I was a Cub Scout. My father would also put on his scout uniform, beaming from ear to ear. I could see the pride in his eyes to be part of this important day. Many people we knew through school soccer, karate, neighbors, etc., would see us, and we would acknowledge each other. I did not even realize 'til much later the positive effect of all this would help dissipate bullying to a large extent. Even though there are at least fifteen Sikh American families that I know in my town and many more in the surrounding towns, in all these years, I have never seen anyone else participate in these special events. No wonder because of such apathy some children have to suffer.

Through scouting on Memorial Day, my brother and I have placed flags on the veterans' graves at the Berlin cemetery for the last few years after attending the parades.[170] Participation on these solemn occasions is important to honor our soldiers, and the side benefit is to assimilate and be accepted by the mainstream. We are doing nothing extra because this is simply good citizenship.

PARTICIPATE IN FUNDRAISING EVENTS

I was part of the "Pink Panther Breast Cancer Team" since 5th grade (2009). We had 7–9 kids, mostly my friends from the same grade, with some dropping out while new ones joined now and again. The first time, we did a fashion show and put on a few ethnic dances with the help of our parents to raise funds. My friend Rahul and I did the "bhangra" with rave reviews. As the years proceeded, I went to our gurdwara to raise money,

---

[170] http://www.troop48berlin.org/content/memorial-day

the local Berlin flea market to sell flags and used stuff, the local gas stations to sell hoagies, sold recipe books to neighbors and my mother's colleagues, and door knocked to raise funds for this great cause. Each year, our entire family would join in the massive turnout in Philadelphia on every Mother's Day to do the 5K walk. The last seven years of unwavering work has helped us raise over $15,000 to make my team the number one high school in the Delaware Valley to raise the most funds. This effort garnered us the Bernie Ashner Award in 2013 and a special commendation in 2015 by the Susan B. Komen Breast Cancer Foundation.[171] We have been featured in several local newspapers and magazines over the years.[172] This kind of work does not go unnoticed by peers and does create goodwill.

Not only did I build a long lasting friendship with my teammates, but they understood the hard work I put in continuously as a co-captain of the team so as to earn their respect. Not only was my team featured in several newspapers and magazines from 2009–2015, my peers in school also became aware of the community service, further earning their respect.[173]

---

[171] http://www.voorheessun.com/2013/09/24/pink-panthers-breast-cancer-team-honored/
http://www.thenjwire.com/2013/sep/10/eastern-regional-high-school-students-raise-thousa/#.UkM5IIaTiSo
https://www.facebook.com/media/set/?set=a.10151546650028325.1073741835.25702638324&type=3#!/photo.php?fbid=10151546666503325&set=a.10151546650028325.1073741835.25702638324&type=3&theater
http://www.courierpostonline.com/article/20130520/NEWS01/305200039/Voorhees-team-takes-part-Komen-event
http://komenphiladelphia.org/race/january-team-news/team-challenges-prizes/
http://site.suburbanfamilymag.com/articles/?articleid=861

[172] http://americansikhcouncil.org/2015/06/page/2/

[173] http://www.courierpostonline.com/article/20130520/NEWS01/305200039/Voorhees-team-takes-part-Komen-event

Co-captain of the Pink Panther Breast Cancer team
with my brother in Philadelphia, PA, May 2015

For the last six years, since 2010, I participated and have raised funds for Multiple Sclerosis (MS) and even biked from Cherry Hill to Mays Landing. This volunteering has been through my Scout troop primarily, but the outreach has been tremendous. At the rest stop in Mays Landing, NJ, over 7,000 cyclists stop to grab water, snacks, and use the restrooms pretty much every year. My brother, father, and I stand out while volunteering for the entire weekend, serving thousands of tired cyclists. On many occasions, cyclists—complete strangers—have asked me about my father's well-being. This can only happen when people see you do good work consistently. This kind of feedback simply makes all the effort even more fulfilling.

At the MS150 bike ride in September 2013,
Mays Landing, NJ, 2nd from right

From 2011–2012, we even participated and raised funds for the March of the Dimes. We also did the 5K walks as they were fun.

VOLUNTEER AT SOUP KITCHENS

When I was younger, my father would take us to the city of Camden to volunteer at one of the soup kitchens. Being involved in multiple activities continuously sometimes made it difficult to do everything, but we still help out at soup kitchens and homeless shelters on occasion.[174] Most recently, my brother, my father, and I went to downtown Philadelphia to serve lunch to the homeless. These activities not only create empathy but keep you humble as it is very easy to forget about others and their suffering.

---

[174] Participated in serving food and cleaning at the Sunday Breakfast Rescue Mission, Philadelphia, on August 15, 2015

My father, my brother, and me with other Sikh American
volunteers at a soup kitchen, August 2015

SIMPLE COMMUNITY SERVICE

The middle school and high school are on either end of my housing development. There are numerous cars driving through our neighborhood, and many simply throw trash out of the windows, which are blown into the bushes, cluttering the storm drains and polluting the pretty lake we have in our neighborhood. It dawned me one evening as I walked back home that I need to something about it. So, once a month on a Friday evening, I would take trash bags and went around collecting the trash, sometimes with my younger brother.

One day, the local police officer stopped me and asked me what I was doing. Once I explained to him that I was simply trying to help clean my community, he complimented me and wished more kids would think of it rather than get into trouble on a Friday evening.

People notice proactive selfless work and goodwill advances in many subtle ways.

SOCIALIZE WITH OTHER FOLKS

It is not uncommon for many in society who will socialize on weekends mostly with their own kind, be it ethnic or religious group. Many places of faith, from churches to temples, are still based on color or ethnicity, though change is slowly taking place. Therefore, it is important that any new person on the block, newer or older immigrant, they must make the effort to socialize with as many different people as possible. Only through social interaction can one break barriers of ignorance and create positive friendships anywhere. Actions must speak louder than words through personal leadership.

Most of my friends are of every major faith, multiple races, and all shades, and that's way I like it. It would be pretty boring if everyone was exactly the same.

ATTEND THE KHALSA SCHOOL

My father planned, organized, and ran the Khalsa school every Sunday from 2004–2007. He was assisted by 2–3 other teachers, and we were taught the "Gurmukhi" script, commonly known as Punjabi language, Sikh history, and explanation of the prayers from the Sikh scripture. There were approximately 35 kids of various age groups but most from 5–15. He divided the kids into groups and rotated 40-minute classes. The two-hour class ran primarily in the basement of the small Gurdwara in Deptford, New Jersey. I was taught the Sikh prayers slowly but surely at home regularly by my parents. Around 2004, when I turned six, the "Sunday school" trips became a fixed feature.

I managed to memorize the morning prayers of 28 pages, and at the age of 8 and since I also got a straight As in school, my parents rewarded me with a "Game Cube." Such rewards helped, and my brother and me managed to memorize the evening and night prayers also. Today, it has become second nature, and I have a greater understanding of the prayers itself. This has helped in keeping me grounded and, hopefully, on the right path.

My father was never harsh or hard; he always explained in a very simple manner so that we could actually understand the basic philosophy of our faith. The heroic stories he told us of the Sikhs who stood against oppression and tyrannies in past few centuries were always fascinating. But he never lectured us, instead walked the walk and talked the talk. He always did everything with us by leading and guiding, by setting an example, and that has been the key to my basic understanding and acceptance of the overall education and the faith.

He found the most well-known and ethically articulate Sikh personalities, soldiers, doctors, athletes, businessmen, etc., across the globe and put up their posters in our room to inspire us. I now realize it did have a psychological effect of perceiving the turban as an asset rather than a hurdle to opportunities out in the world. I have certainly become an optimistic person.

'Til the age of 11, the last thing, while wishing us goodnight, my father would make us say something inspiring like "impossible is nothing"! He would change that every now and then, and we had to repeat it while I would find it amusing. Today, I understand that the silly thing I repeated actually psyched us up to be stronger and have a more positive outlook to life.

My father read hundreds of books while teaching Sikh theology and history so that he could give us the most accurate and balanced information possible. In the bargain, he ended up compiling an excellent book list for Sikh children which has been vetted by the national council and is now used by thousands of parents and children across the nation.[175]

There was some personalities in the Deptford gurdwara who were just jealous of all the good work my father continued to do, and a few started to patronizingly mock him, even though he was teaching their children too! He saw the writing on the wall, and in September 2007, we switched to a different Khalsa school which was located in Lawrenceville, NJ. There were over a hundred kids of mostly parents who were professionals. The school had at least eighteen volunteer teachers. My father did not have to help as much, but he continued to teach us at home, in addition to the Sunday school. From 2007–2013, I regularly attended classes, and I can personally

---

[175] http://www.worldsikhcouncil.org/educmat/books.html

attest to the fact that it was worth the 85-mile round trip every Sunday for more than six years.

What my father did since I turned thirteen was even more interesting. My brother and I would come up with a question once a week, and then all of us would browse through the various scriptures of other faiths and our own to find the answers. In the process, we learnt about other faiths and figured out which had the best answers to our varied questions. This gave us a hands-on look at other faiths to gain a healthy respect for other religions.

Even though my parents were a little reluctant because of my age, I impressed upon them that I understand the commitment and insisted on going forward; so, in April 2014, I went through the formal initiation ceremony to take "Khande Da Phaul."[176] This did not happen overnight but through the diligent education and love displayed by my parents, which gave me the impetus and confidence to take the next step in my life.

At the ground breaking ceremony at the Sikh Sabha Gurdwara,
Lawrenceville, NJ (2nd from right)

---

[176] The formal Sikh – 'Khande Da Phaul' ceremony, in order to become a Khalsa

ATTEND THE SIKH CAMPS

My father ran the Sikh summer camp at the Deptford Gurdwara from 2002–2007. He took an entire week of time off from work and helped organize and smoothly run the week-long camp for 50-plus kids for five years. It took a lot of effort because he was one of the few men who diligently compiled a camp manual and tried to run it professionally. It was so much fun as we got to play games in the afternoon and hung out with friends. At the end of the week, we went to Sikh Flags Great Adventure Park, Hershey Park, or Clementon Park for an all-day outing. The camps were a crash course on quite a bit of what we learnt during the year, but for many, this was the only time they learnt anything about their religious heritage, and it certainly wasn't enough to make an impact since many did not attend the regular Sunday classes.

From 2007–2009, my father took us to the week-long camp at the Philadelphia Sikh Society Gurdwara in Millbourne, PA.

Starting in 2009, my brother and I attended "Camp Khanda" in Syracuse, NY, where my father taught history and stayed with us for the entire time. He also took kids hiking and fishing. The younger kids went nuts as he taught them how to fish, tie knots, and catch their first fish. As I grew, I did the same and started to help the younger kids. The camp had between 40–50 kids from all over the country but primarily from the East Coast for most years.

At "Camp Khanda," the kirtan teacher was awesome as she taught my brother and me "shabds" very quickly and easily without going through the long-winded fundamentals.[177] Aunty Manjot was polite and knew how to handle kids without ever raising her voice. In the past several years, I have learnt many "shabds," all thanks to her guidance.[178] The adults at this camp were all professionals with advanced degrees and a passion to pass on the Sikh heritage. This surely helped because every one of them had something new to add, so we came back home, recharged and rearing to go.

---

[177] Mrs.Manjot Kaur Saini of the Khalsa School, Brampton, Ontario, Canada

[178] Shabds – hymns from the Sikh scripture – Shri Guru Granth Sahib

As I enter my junior year in high school, I was nominated to be a junior counselor for the summer camp. The kids in my group were all bright, many on the top of their class and ambitious, so to get picked was an honor.

These Sikh camps are not only educational but build lifelong networks with others from within the faith community, which could never happen otherwise since most live across the nation with little chance of running into each other.

These camps have helped build the next-level organizations such as "Surat," which have once-a-year conferences held by mostly Sikh American college students, who not only discuss important current issues challenging the community but also network on the side for various reasons, from business to love.[179] There is also "Saanjh," which is similar to "Surat," held primarily on the West Coast. These being safe spaces, long-term friendships are shaped, which also strengthen one's faith, are important to mature emotionally and otherwise.[180]

INCLUSION OF THE SUSTAINED THIRD SIKH GENOCIDE IN SCHOOLS

My father has worked diligently and closely with the New Jersey Commission of Holocaust Education for over ten years. This monumental effort finally paid off, and starting in December 2014, all information about the Third Sikh Genocide is now accessible as teaching material for dissemination across the state of New Jersey so that students from elementary school to high school can learn and be made aware about the atrocities perpetuated on the Sikhs in Punjab and elsewhere across India through the Sustained Sikh Genocide from 1984–1998 in which over one million Sikhs were raped, murdered, and made to disappear by the Indian regime.

This landmark move by the New Jersey Commission on Holocaust Education to include the teaching of the Sustained Third Sikh Genocide (1984–1998) (www.thirdsikhgenocide.org) in all the schools across the State of New Jersey is, indeed, historic.

---

[179] http://www.thesuratinitiative.com/

[180] http://www.saanjh.org/

I saw my father patiently work on this project for years, making phone calls for hours, then traveling to meet officials, and finally, in December 2014, he got a phone call from the person in charge, followed by an official letter from the head of the New Jersey Commission on Holocaust Education, making the Sikh Genocide of 1984–1998 a permanent part of the "Holocaust and other Genocides" in the state's educational curriculum. I could see the joy and elation in my father of trying to help his faith community to gain some semblance of justice. This was all thanks to my father's incredible selfless work which made this happen.

The New Jersey Holocaust Commission, in conjunction with the New Jersey Department of Education, is to be applauded for taking this noble step to help educate school children about others around them. This momentous step will not only educate all children but reduce ignorance, create genuine respect, and hopefully reduce bullying of Sikh American children.

(http://www.state.nj.us/education/holocaust/resources/)

A BULLYING EXAMPLE FROM MY SCHOOL

In the previous chapter on "Psychological Trauma," I gave an example of Harneel being bullied from K–12, a few years my senior in the same school. Here, I want to use his example and show you how some of my proactive solutions have worked in my favor and foiling any attempts of bullying against me or my brother so far.

Harneel was never involved in any martial arts, boy scouts, public speaking, community service in the town, or any other activity which could build his self-confidence and camaraderie outside of school within the local community. His parents were never involved in the school activities or in any local community events. Even the learning of the Sikh faith or the heritage was of a minimal level. These are all very critically important activities which were missing from Harneel's skill set to tackle the incessant bullying trauma he went through.

All the above-mentioned activities, when systematically inculcated over years, has a tremendous effect on the child in building a strong foundation of knowledge, high self-esteem, solid self-confidence, a large network of peers who see you as part of them rather than the "outsider," a person to be taken seriously who is not a pushover, good social/interpersonal skills, and an extrovert. Parents have to put in a tremendous of time in long-term planning, time, and money to do all the above as these also happen to be excellent life skills which simultaneously help tackle bulling very effectively.

My father did try politely to have Harneel's father involve his son in all the above activities, including asking him to become a soccer coach so that he could help his son(s) just like my father was doing, but he claimed he did not have the time, and that was the end of it.

Furthermore, there were at least three turbaned Sikh kids who went through the same school I attend prior to Harneel.[181] Teachers and students were aware of Sikhs prior to Harneel since the three students who graduated earlier were fairly articulate, extroverted, and ended up going to and graduating from top-notch universities.[182] So, part of the problem was in the way Harneel carried and handled himself among his peers without having all the life skills to prepare him for the school environment and beyond.[183]

HANDLING AND REPORTING ABUSE

If parents find that no amount of complaints about bullying to the school authorities stopping it, then the next logical step is to file a formal complaint to the appropriate state Human Relations Commission to prompt an investigation. Typically, no school wants the notoriety which goes with

---

[181] Between 1999–2010, the year before Harneel Singh Saini graduated, the three Sikh kids were Tony Singh Rahil, who graduated in 2000; Dr. Pritpaul Singh's son, who graduated sometime in 2002; and finally, Sandeep Singh Guleria, who graduated in 2006 from Eastern High School, Voorhees, NJ.

[182] Guleria from New York University, Rahil from Brown University, and the third one from Temple University.

[183] He could not even tie his patka (little turban) on his own 'til he was 16–17 years old. This is something very basic which is taught by parents to their children by the age of 12–13, normally, in order to be self-sufficient, not be dependent on anyone, and gain self-confidence.

an investigation from the state authorities and very likely will take action to stop the bullying, regardless of their personal feelings.

A complaint to the Division of Civil Rights can also prompt some serious action, waking up any school which has been lazy or noncompliant to a zero tolerance policy.

Sikh American advocacy organizations like Sikh Coalition and SALDEF can be approached as they are pretty active in assisting bullied children.

COOL SIKH COMIC(S)

In early 2015, a Sikh American, Supreet Singh Manchanda, came out with a brand new comic superhero named "Deep Singh," who is a "Sikh–James Bond" of sorts.[184] Through a Kickstarter campaign, they were able to raise over $22,000 to bring out the first issue. Comic books are iconic and have been a staple diet of kids the world over for the last century. Introducing a Sikh superhero into the American mainstream will have a tremendous effect in educating and putting a positive spin on a faith which has been misunderstood because of various reasons.

Super Sikh, the first Sikh American superhero

---

[184] http://sanfrancisco.cbslocal.com/2015/02/25/bay-area-comic-book-writers-introduce-first-sikh-super-hero-who-loves-elvis/

There have been some turban-wearing characters in comic books earlier, albeit a few, and those have been "Muslim-looking" in some cases, with "Muslim names" in many cases, but extremely few with actual Sikh names.[185] Aside from the issue of political correctness, cartoonists in most cases have actually done a bad job of depicting a particular character appropriately, instead creating more confusion.

So, the addition of this new Sikh superhero into the world of comic books would, indeed, alleviate ignorance—but to what extent is to be seen. I, for one, hope that it will be positive in educating, inspiring, and reducing bullying!

SIKH CARTOONS

Sikhs have a great sense of humor and are one of those faith groups who can also laugh at themselves. Unfortunately, there are many other faith groups who do not carry the same self-esteem in order to laugh at themselves that easily.

Vishavajit Singh, the creator of "Sikhtoons," is probably the most uncharacteristic individual to be a likely cartoonist. Yet this very smart, unassuming, humble, and witty man has made a name for himself as a well-respected cartoonist.[186] Vishvajit Singh's cartoons are about many issues, from school bullying, to political satire, to human right violations, and much more. Thanks to the Internet, many non-Sikhs have started to view and slowly understand the Sikhs.

---

[185] http://www.comicbookreligion.com/

[186] http://www.sikhtoons.com/

DRESSING UP CAPTAIN AMERICA FOR A MISSION

TURBAN PURCHASED FROM SOUTHALL, LONDON

THE A THREADED OUT OF THE CAPTAIN AMERICA COSTUME CAP SKILLFULLY BY MY WIFE AND PINNED TO THE TURBAN

CAPTAIN AMERICA: WINTER SOLDIER INSPIRED COSTUME AVAILABLE IN LARGE SIZE ONLY PURCHASED FROM AN ONLINE VENDOR.

SHOULDERS, ARMS, CHEST, WAIST, LEGS, INSEAM ALTERED TO FIT SIZE SMALL AT DE JAVU BOUTIQUE IN NYC

24 INCH SHIELD PURCHASED FROM ANOTHER ONLINE VENDOR

CAPTAIN AMERICA SHIELD BUCKLE BELT PURCHASED FROM A BANGLADESHI STREET VENDOR IN CHINATOWN, NYC

PAIR OF SUPRA SOCIETY S SHOES WITH HIP HOP INSPIRED DESIGN

SIKHTOONS.COM

Vishavajit Singh has created a cult following among Sikhs
and others across the nation and globally

On September 10, 2013, Vishvajit Singh came up with a novel idea by becoming a comic book character. He dressed up as Captain America—spandex, shield, and, of course, the iconic turban! Like Vishavjit puts it, "I wore that costume to challenge the way New Yorkers think about superheroes—and bearded Sikhs like me"![187] Now, here is a 120-pound, skinny Sikh American who literally put himself out in front of the public in America's most populous city, ready to take on the racism and compliments in his stride, simply in a valiant attempt to educate and reduce

[187] http://www.salon.com/2013/09/10/captain_america_in_a_turban/

183

bigotry. In my book, he is a genuine hero, trying to make a difference—a real "American"![188]

Dalbir Singh of Sikh Park captures the essence of preconceived perceptions

Another cartoonist who is not as well-known as Vishvajit Singh is Dalbir Singh, creator of "Sikh Park," a play on "South Park."[189] His cartoons are entertaining, nonetheless, and deal with everyday humor and are lighter than "Sikhtoons." These men are trailblazers in their fields, inspiring thousands of kids, educating, creating awareness, putting a smile on millions of faces, and, most of all, making a statement that we add something unique to the flavor of humanity. I can assure you the world would be pretty boring without us.

YOUTUBE COMEDIANS

There is a genre of comedians who were born and grew up in North America by creating a name for themselves through YouTube videos. Jasmeet Singh, aka Jus Reign, is one of the hottest male Sikh Canadian comedians at the moment with over 1 million hits regularly on YouTube.[190] According to his own Jus Reign Wikia, "Jus Reign was born in a small town in Canada, Toronto on the November 4th 1989 living with his Mum, Dad, two younger brothers, Gran and Grandad and his four uncles in the one household. When Jasmeet Singh went to school everyone else who was in his school always questioned what was on his head (Turban) which made Jasmeet feel very different to society back then."[191] Jasmeet has used humor to the hilt in order to make the turban cool and a nonissue by educating everyone around him. His style of wit, sarcasm, self-deprecating humor has gone a long way to breaking down many barriers since the new world learns a lot from and through the Internet.

Jasmeet Singh, aka Jus Reign

[190] https://www.facebook.com/JusReign 1,077,635 likes on August 24, 2015
[191] http://jusreign.wikia.com/wiki/JusReign

CONCLUSION

There are a many life-skill tools available and most are just common sense. The problem is that most parents either find all the above propositions too cumbersome because they are either lazy, or they have excuses that they do not have enough time and/or they do not have the means. The decision for a parent is pretty straightforward—is your child a priority? If your child is a priority and you want him/her to do fantastically well without any bullying, then some, if not most, of the suggested practical solutions used by me should be adopted and incorporated into the child's daily regimen in order for them to live and lead a life with their head held high to hopefully have a life with fewer bumps in the road. There are no shortcuts. It is a long road, but as long as you persevere, you will make it, but you have still have to the plan and work at it.

STRATEGIES FOR EDUCATORS

"Never believe that a few caring people can't change the world.
For, indeed, that's all who ever have."
Margaret Mead[192]

ADMINISTRATORS AND TEACHERS

The adults running and teaching in all the schools have a very big responsibility in supervising and implementing discipline. It is never easy or simple to control hundreds to thousands of children from ages 5–18 inside a school environment. Nevertheless, it behooves that the administrators and teachers to keep an eagle eye on bullying of any kind but also be mature and unbiased enough to define or delineate bullying in order to stop it.

Administrators and teachers also need to be trained in racial/religious diversity sensitivity as, after all, they are humans too and can be ignorant. I remember my parents, while having a parent–teacher conference, asking my brother's 3rd grade teacher[193] at Osage Elementary School if she knew what faith we professed sometime in 2006. She did not have an answer and was clueless. It is a general epidemic in the educational arena, i.e., for generations we have been conditioned on minimal education about world history, world religions, and world geography. This endemic issue

---

[192] http://www.brainyquote.com/quotes/topics/topic_change.html#50jR351M0w WAD2A8.99

[193] Mrs. Recca was a very nice and polite teacher.

is one of the foundational problems which is actually a lack of education, therefore, ignorance, firstly among adults and then among children. The state curricula setting bodies seem to be largely living in an insular world where the assumption is that the audience they are catering to is largely "white, Anglo-Saxon, Eurocentric"; therefore, there is no need to change quickly. Furthermore, 'til the recent past, most of public was happy in the fact that there is us (America) and then the rest of the world. Somehow, we Americans are insulated and completely separate from the rest. No wonder we have the World Series in baseball with only Americans competing in it! Where is the rest of the world? This peculiar mindset has to change fast because the world has changed rapidly, especially with the advent of the Internet in the last twenty-plus years.

The fact is that by 2050, all minorities are going to be in the majority at 54%.[194] There are 500,000 immigrants who come into the US legally from all over the globe every year. In the state of California, the "white" population stands at 39% and are already in the minority.[195] Without looking into any kind of alarmist racial overtones, this is simply the ground reality and must be dealt with in a mature, systematic way so that everyone can be genuinely "respected" equally and not simply tolerated in a haphazard manner.

On the 10th anniversary of the attack on the Twin Towers in New York City, my father was invited to speak as one of the speakers to address the children in my school in September 2011. My father, who was originally invited for one session, ended up staying to address the entire middle school all day upon the request by the principal, Dr. Diane Young, and diversity director, Ms. Irene Afek. Kids were brought into the main library in large groups, and one of the key questions he asked at every session was if anyone could tell him what faith he professed. Out of the over 1,100 children, not a single one gave the correct answer. I was present at one of his speaking sessions that day and was disappointedly amazed at the ignorance. This is in spite of the fact that my father had given presentations in 2007 to the

---

[194] http://www.nytimes.com/imagepages/2008/08/14/washington/14census.ready.html

[195] http://www.ppic.org/main/publication_show.asp?i=259

entire Osage Elementary School consisting of over 550 children, the entire Voorhees school administration in 2009, and the many smaller interactions in the same vein in between. This simply goes to show the apathy by the administrators and teachers not being able to teach such a simple fact to all the students, which could stop bullying in its tracks to a large extent of Sikh American children. If a middle school child does not have the education to first know what faith his/her peer belongs to and secondly what "that particular faith stands for, it becomes doubly difficult for the bullied child to explain while being traumatized."

The homogeneity of the teachers is another issue which plays into the overall scheme. Unless and until the administrators and teachers are a close reflection of the diversity in the classrooms, it becomes a challenge for "others" to truly understand the subtle nuances of ethnic/religious challenges a child goes through on a daily basis.[196]

Lack of information regarding major faith groups and, particularly, the Sikh faith in the school Social Studies books across the nation is still a monumental challenge. This is one of the fundamental issues which have been the bane of the Sikh faith community. Today's 6th grade Social Studies books typically contain all basic information about the Christian, Jewish, Buddhist, Muslim, and even the Hindu faiths. But there is nothing anywhere about the Sikh faith, even though Sikh Americans have lived here since the late 19th century.

CALIFORNIA'S CURRICULUM FRAMEWORK TIMELINE

In California, Dr. Onkar Singh Bindra, an alumni of the University of California, Berkeley, a retired entomologist, spearheaded a campaign for years with help of several individuals, gurdwaras, and other Sikh organizations to include information about the "Sikhs," initially, in the 6th grade Social Studies book.[197]

---

[196] http://www.edtechpolicy.org/ArchivedWebsites/chisholm.htm

[197] http://www.sikhcoalition.org/advisories/2012/governor-signs-bill-that-allows-curriculum-process-to-move-forward

Since 2010, the Sikh Coalition has supported three different bills that were introduced in both the Assembly and Senate to ensure that the draft framework could be completed.

California Governor Jerry Brown signed a bill in 2013 which significantly raises hopes that public school children will learn about the Sikhs in California sooner than later.

The bill, Senate Bill 1540, grants state education officials permission to complete a near-finished draft of the state's History–Social Science "framework." This framework provides teachers with the information they need in order to teach students the content standards for each subject area. The current draft framework includes seven references to Sikhs, including Guru Nanak, Sikh immigrants and their struggles, Dalip Singh Saund (the first Sikh American three-term congressman), and Bhagat Singh Thind (the first Sikh American turban-wearing soldier in the US Army, who also was a trail-blazing pioneer for citizenship and property rights for all Asian Americans).

Now that SB 1540 has been signed, this draft framework can be completed. It is my hope that the Sikh examples that are currently included will remain in the final version.[198]

The timeline below chronicles the efforts of the Sikh Coalition, several individuals, a few Bay Area gurdwaras guided by Dr. Onkar Singh Bindra to make this happen.

- July 17, 2009 – A committee of teachers and other educators appointed by the State Board of Education had been meeting to review the current History–Social Science curriculum framework and to recommend revisions. On this day, several Sikh examples are included in the draft History–Social Science framework.

---

[198] The Sikh Coalition would like to recognize Dr. Onkar Singh Bindra (Sacramento) for championing this important achievement. Dr. Bindra worked with countless State Assembly members and senators to ask that Sikhs be included in California's school curriculum. The Sikh Coalition sincerely thanks Dr. Bindra for his leadership.

- July 28, 2009 – Governor Schwarzenegger signs a bill which stops all work on instructional material adoptions and curriculum framework revisions effective immediately and continuing until the 2013–14 school year. This suspends any further action on the History–Social Science framework revision process.

- February 18, 2010 – The Coalition's first attempt: Upon Dr. Bindra's urging, a bill is proposed by Assembly Member Carter which calls for an adoption of the revised History–Social Science Framework. At Dr. Bindra's request, the Sikh Coalition reaches out to the Chair of Assembly Appropriations Committee to pass this bill when it arrives in this committee. Unfortunately, this bill did not pass out of the Assembly Appropriations Committee.

- February 19, 2010 – The Coalition's second attempt: At Dr. Bindra's request, the Sikh Coalition supports a Senate bill asking that the curriculum framework be adopted. The Coalition writes letters of support and places phone calls to the Senate Education Committee, Assembly Education Committee, as well as the Assembly Appropriations Committee, to pass it. This bill would also require the State Board of Education to adopt the revised curriculum framework for History–Social Science and Science in 2011. In addition, the Coalition sends emails to California Sikhs urging them to support this bill and calling them to action. Unfortunately, this bill did not pass out of the Assembly Appropriations Committee either.

- February 24, 2012 – The Coalition's third attempt: Since the prior two bills had died, Dr. Bindra approaches Senator Hancock to introduce SB 1540. She did, along with five coauthors. SB 1540 would resume the unfinished work on the History–Social Science framework and see it through to completion. The Coalition writes a letter of support to Senator Hancock.

- August 23, 2012 – SB 1540 passes through the California Assembly and Senate and is now on the governor's desk. The Sikh Coalition creates an online petition and letter-writing campaign for California constituents to contact the governor, urging him to sign this bill. The Coalition delivered close to 500 petition signatures to the governor's office.

- August 1–September 7, 2012 – The Secretary General, Kavneet Singh, representing the American Sikh Council, formerly known as World Sikh Council - America Region, spent quite a bit of time and called several gurdwaras' representatives to garner backing and finally called all the relevant legislators to get their support.
- September 8, 2012 – Governor Brown signs SB 1540, allowing the Curriculum Commission to complete the revision process of the draft History–Social Science Curriculum framework which includes Sikhs in seven distinct areas in the framework.[199]

After years of lobbying by various individual Sikhs like Dr. Onkar Singh Bindra,[200] advocacy organizations like the Sikh Coalition,[201] and a few Bay Area gurdwaras,[202] a law got passed in the state of California to include information about the "Sikhs" in the social studies and history books from elementary to high school. The final Bill SB1540 (Hancock) was signed by Governor Jerry Brown on September 8, 2012.[203] There was another important bill—namely, AB1964, the "Workplace Religious Freedom Act"—introduced by Assemblywoman Mrs. Mariko Yamada and supported by a variety of faith groups, including Catholics, Muslims, Jews, and Sikhs, considered a landmark legislation in protecting civil rights of Americans

---

[199] http://www.sikhcoalition.org/advisories/2012/governor-signs-bill-that-allows-curriculum-process-to-move-forward#sthash.jDpRVbhM.dpuf

[200] A retired entomologist who taught in India and Nigeria but eventually retired to live close to his children in San Francisco, CA. He holds a doctorate from the University of California at Berkley, CA.

[201] Sikh Coalition is run by a group of 5–8 passionate youngish attorneys with two offices: one in Manhattan, NY, and the other in Fremont, CA. The entire staff is salaried with very few unpaid volunteers. Their annual budget runs approximately $1.5 million dollars. Collecting funds constantly is imperative, otherwise the staff cannot be paid; therefore, sharing the spotlight with other much larger umbrella organizations, such as the American Sikh Council, becomes problematic for them and others like them.

[202] Sikh Gurdwara, San Jose, CA; Gurdwara Sahib, Fremont, CA; Gurdwara Sahib El Sobrante, CA; Pacific Coast Khalsa Diwan, Stockton, CA; Sacramento Sikh Society, Sacramento, CA

[203] https://brownpolitics.wordpress.com/tag/sb-1540/

of all backgrounds.[204] Not only did the secretary general of the American Sikh Council write letters to at least sixteen California state legislatures on behalf of the American Sikh Council[205] but, in 2012, followed it up by calling each one of them just before voting to make sure they understood the momentous significance of the bill for Sikh Americans. This was a hard-won victory for Sikh Americans after a very long time.

The last detailed public review meeting held in Sacramento, CA, was December 18–19, 2014.[206] This meeting was one of a series of many ongoing meetings held in reference to the inclusion of content relating to the Sikh faith, history, culture, and contribution of Sikh Americans to the United States of America.

The American Sikh Council recently sent a strongly worded letter out to the California State Board of Education, alerting them on the clever machinations of a few non-Sikh interest groups. The Board of Education is cognizant of the fact that the Sikh Americans are facing the issue of ignorance by their co-citizens, but they have a bureaucratic structure to work with, allowing all kinds of interest groups, from the genuine to the extreme right wing, who are challenging literally every word that has been written in these textbooks. It is, therefore, up to all proactive Sikh organizations to broach this issue as one monolith in order to tackle this attack.

There seems to have been quite a bit of positive progress made at the most recent public interest meeting held in Sacramento, CA, by the California Department of Education on October 8, 2015. In this meeting, many suggested changes by Sikh organizations and the American Sikh Council were adopted as is. My fervent hope is that accurate content on the Sikh American heritage and contribution be published soon so that children can hold their head high and be regarded as equals without being bullied.

---

[204] http://www.examiner.com/article/governor-jerry-brown-carves-his-name-history-by-signing-ab-1964-and-sb-1540

[205] Formerly known as World Sikh Council - America Region (WSC-AR) www.worldsikhcouncil.org Secretary General – Kavneet Singh

[206] There was a more recent meeting held on June 4, 2015, which was not attended by all the Sikh representatives in Sacramento, CA.

INCLUDE SIKH FAITH IN THE SCHOOL CURRICULA

Unless and until information about the Sikh faith, the history, and contribution of the Sikh Americans is included in all the social studies and history books in all fifty states across our nation, the pervasive ignorance will continue.

A small community can only do so much with limited resources; otherwise, a concerned adult's entire time is taken up by educating everyone around them and ending up doing nothing else. It can be overwhelming at times as I saw that happen on rare occasions with my father. The boards of education in every state are keenly aware of the fact that the information on the "Sikh faith" is missing from the curriculum. It behooves right-minded educators to include the relevant information sooner than later as every day that goes by, some child somewhere in America is being badly bullied, leaving lifelong scars on innocent children.

SIKH GENOCIDE AWARENESS

Like I mentioned earlier, content about the Jewish Holocaust is mandatory and taught in all schools across several states in our country, which include New Jersey, Florida, Illinois, California, New York, and Pennsylvania.[207] Now that the preliminary content about the Sustained Sikh Genocide 1984–1998 has been included in the Holocaust and Genocide studies in the state of New Jersey, the same should be adopted by other states. Genocide studies should include all genocides across the globe as America has citizens from every ethnic background, religious group, and country. This would only enhance education and create more awareness, hopefully generating empathy and reducing bullying.

My dad planned and organized the first conference of its kind on the Sustained Sikh Genocide 1984–1998, which was held at Princeton University, New Jersey, on February 7, 2015.[208] The crux of the conference

---

[207] https://en.wikipedia.org/wiki/Laws_requiring_teaching_of_the_Holocaust

[208] http://planetprinceton.com/event/conference-on-sikh-genocide-in-india-at-princeton-university/

was to bring about awareness and educate the educators about this relatively unknown pogrom. Teachers specializing in history and social studies were invited, including professors from local universities, who really appreciated the eye-opening factual information. These are some small steps toward indirectly reducing bullying.

Educators need to hold conferences covering Sikh and other genocides on a regular basis so that children are conscious of the pain and suffering of other humans. The New Jersey Commission on Holocaust Education is already working diligently toward doing exactly what I am suggesting.[209]

BOY SCOUTS OF AMERICA WORKBOOKS

My father had been planning for years to find an alternate method to providing information about the Sikhs to the same school-going children who were not getting the information through the regular school text-books. Since getting each state to rectify and include the content on the Sikhs amounted to a full-time task and a long uphill battle with a lot of bureaucratic red tape, he came up with a plan to circumvent the system and do it his way.

In and around late 2006, he started to inquire about the process of getting a workbook which contained the basic information about the Sikhs approved by the Boy Scouts of America (BSA). He made many phone calls, met many adult Scout leaders in southern New Jersey, eventually making some headway by 2011. It took over five long years just to figure out the system and process, and all the while, he was juggling many other things. During this period, he had been serving as a nominated volunteer on the American Sikh Council board off and on over the years.[210] After much planning with the exceptional support of Kirpal Singh Nijher, a former chairperson of the same council, he was able to spearhead the first workbook. Starting in 2012 with one book, within the next two years, he

---

[209] http://www.state.nj.us/education/holocaust/

[210] American Sikh Council (ASC) (www.americansikhcouncil.org), formerly known as the World Sikh Council - America Region (www.worldsikhcouncil.org), a national association of over 68 Gurdwaras and Sikh institutions across the US.

was able to complete four separate workbooks meant for children grades 1–12.[211] My brother and I went through the book drafts constantly, giving input and ideas because they were geared toward our age group.

The Sikh Religious Awards workbooks contained various levels of content pertaining to the Sikh faith, a little history, the language, but overall providing enough information that even an adult can get enough information to understand the basic concepts very clearly about a much maligned, much misunderstood community. All the workbooks were fully approved by Boy Scouts of America, and the best part is that the books were designed to teach the general audience, including the Sikh American children in and out of their Sunday religious classes. The seasoned hand helping my father patiently at BSA was none other than Mr. Wray Johanning, guiding with his wisdom and wit. If more men of vision and understanding were like Mr. Johanning, the world would be a more peaceful place with less bullying.

---

[211] http://americansikhcouncil.org/2013/11/05/boy-scouts-of-america-approves-sikh-religious-award-in-consultation-with-wsc-ar/

Sikh Religious Awards Study Workbook Grades 9–12 youth

American Sikh Council

www.americansikhcouncil.org

The cover of one of the four SRA workbooks approved by the BSA

In the May 2015 issue of *Boy's Life*, all the four Sikh Religious Awards (SRA) workbooks and the accompanying emblems were featured beautifully, going out to over 1.1 million Scouts across the nation.[212]

---

[212] http://americansikhcouncil.org/2015/05/03/sikh-religious-emblems-featured-in-boys-life-magzine/

Article in the Boy Scouts Scouting magazine, *Boy's Life*, May 2015 issue

Today, whenever anyone completes the Sikh Religious Awards workbook, four striking metal emblems are awarded for the four levels, accompanied with a certificate of completion. These can be done by anybody 'til the age of eighteen, of any faith or no faith, in scouts or out of scouts. Thanks to my father's ingenuity and dogged perseverance, millions of Boy Scouts and Girl Scouts are now becoming aware of these workbooks and emblems. Hopefully, this multipronged strategy will pay great dividends as more children start working on these books by educating themselves, dispelling ignorance, creating more goodwill, and reducing the level of bullying across the nation.

My brother and me were the first two kids to complete the SRA workbooks and received our emblems in July of 2014.[213] Today, many other scouts from troops across the country and non-scouts have completed and others in the process of working on these workbooks.

Thanks to eight years of work my father put in to complete this momentous project, today there is content available on the Sikhs which can be used by any child anywhere to inform them of a unique people and earn an emblem/medallion in the process.

My father, who never tires of coming up with more stuff to educate others, so he worked with Mr. Kirpal Singh Nijher and came out with a great tri-fold brochure to educate anyone, called "Sikhs and Scouts."[214] This tri-fold brochure is also approved by the Boy Scouts of America and is available on their website, as well as on the Internet, readily downloadable. In the meanwhile, the Boy Scouts of America have printed 17,000 of these to disseminate across the country. Sikh American kids and anyone interested should use these to educate others or themselves as it is the simple and easy to understand.

In 2014, my father, along with Mr. Kirpal Singh Nijher and Mrs. Jasbir Kaur Bhullar, contributed content on the Sikh faith in a brand new book called *Scouting Our Way: A Guide to Faith, Duty and Fellowship*, published by Dr. Robert Lee Edmonds and Mrs. Linda Tucker Edmonds in the spring

---

[213] http://americansikhcouncil.org/2014/08/06/sikh-scouts-receive-first-sikh-rel igious-awards-approved-by-boy-scouts-of-america/

[214] http://www.scouting.org/filestore/membership/pdf/Sikhs_and_Scouts.pdf

of 2015.[215] *Scouting Our Way* (www.scoutingourway.com) contains prayers under three subheadings—namely, Duty to God, Duty to Self, and Duty to Others—with a prominent photograph of my brother and me, both Eagle Scouts. Prayers from various faiths are included in a simple yet beautiful manner, creating a commonality and universal brotherhood while trying to follow the Creator through responsible citizenship. A must-have book for anyone wanting to learn about diversity and kinship. The book is being put on every Scout Council store shelf across the nation as we speak and is also available on Amazon, all thanks to Dr. Edmonds' phenomenal work.

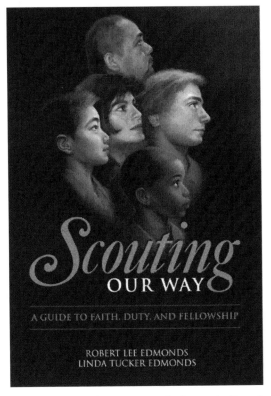

Scouting book with prayers from various faiths, including the Sikh faith

---

[215] http://www.amazon.com/Scouting-Our-Way-Guide-Fellowship/dp/0989202607/ref=sr_1_2?s=books&ie=UTF8&qid=1442086247&sr=1-2

In late December 2012, my father took time off to plan and lead the first ever Sikh American contingent to participate in the National Boy Scouts Jamboree held at the Bechtel Summit, Mt. Hope, West Virginia, in July–August 2013. I assisted my father to fundraise and come up with ideas to implement at the Sikh Faith and Beliefs exhibit.

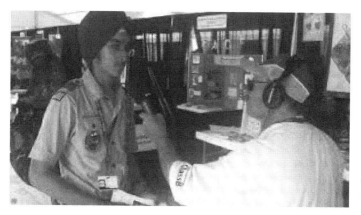

Being interviewed by a radio station host at the Boy Scouts
Jamboree on July 17, 2013

We drove 500 miles each way from southern New Jersey to the 10,000-acre campsite. My father, my younger brother, seven other adults, and I spent 12 days in total manning the exhibit at the Jamboree. It was the most incredible experience of my life so far! Interacting with my peers from across the nation and some across the world gave me a unique perspective because the reaction of pretty much most of the Scouts was most humbling. Everyone was so nice and respectful as it was hard to imagine so many well-mannered people in one place. All of us must have tied over 1,500 turbans on anyone wanting one tied. We actually ran out of turban cloth, eventually, as all the kids wanted to keep them as souvenirs and we let them. The kids were not only thrilled to tie the turbans, but they did not remove them all day and thought it was the coolest thing ever.

Some of the adult Sikh representatives with Scouts
beaming ear to ear in brand new turbans

I could not imagine that complete strangers would be so respectful toward an intimate piece of clothing which is an article of faith for me. This experience cannot be described but had to be felt to understand as to how genuine interaction with others can change them but also make me a better human being, simultaneously making me proud of my heritage.

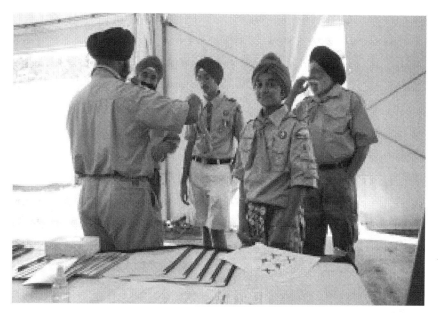

Setting up the exhibit with my father and brother

One of our first visitors to the exhibit

Start of the Jamboree at the exhibit with my brother

Several Scouts and adult leaders with me in turbans

Talking and interacting with fellow Scouts

Tying a turban on a Scout from Seattle at the exhibit

As an Eagle Scout, my brother and me spoke to hundreds upon hundreds of Boy Scouts and adult leaders, all the while explaining about our faith and history. I have never spoken to so many people in such a short time. We gave out thousands of the "Sikhs and Scouts" tri-fold brochures which was designed by my father.[216] I had the privilege to meet the Chief Scout, Mr. Wayne Brock, and the Chair of the Jamboree, Mr. Charles Dalquist, and his colleague Mr. Henry Sorensen. They personally complimented my brother and me for showing true leadership at the ten-day Jamboree event.

All children, but especially Sikh American children, are missing out on the most rewarding and fun program from ages 6–18 ever devised all for a pittance. The Boy Scout/Girl Scout programs are a giant bag of life skills, many of which are taught in corporate America to adults. There is so much a child can do that you will run out of energy but rarely be able to do everything the entire program has to offer. My family is one example. I have completed Eagle at age 14 just before I turned 15, but my younger brother finished his Eagle at age 12 years and 10 months, so he decided to keep going and is working on completing the Hornaday Award at the moment. Not to be left behind, my father finished his Wood Badge in August 2015 while he is an Assistant Scoutmaster of our Troop. He also chairs the Boy Scout Task Force, along with being the Secretary General of the American Sikh Council and a member of the Religious Beliefs and Emblems Task Force of the Boy Scouts of America.

This is an awesome way to interact, make friends, assimilate, learn, have fun, enjoy the beautiful environment, and have an adventure every time. If you are not in Scouts, you will have regrets—if you only knew how incredibly cool it is—since this is simply the best bang for the buck, without a doubt.

RECRUITMENT IN THE US ARMED FORCES

The ultimate patriotism for any American is to serve his/her country in the Armed Forces. The Sikh Americans, primarily because of their faith, would join the US Armed Forces in droves if given an opportunity. The

---

[216] http://www.scouting.org/filestore/membership/pdf/Sikhs_and_Scouts.pdf

Sikh American recruitment would be higher than anyone else versus their percentage in the overall population, and there is ample evidence to substantiate this rather unusual fact. 'Til 1947, the Sikhs made up over 35% of the British Indian Armed Forces when their actual percentage against the rest of the population was less than 2%.[217]

"In the last two World Wars, 83,000 turban wearing Sikh soldiers were killed and 109,045 wounded for the freedom of Britain and the world during shell fire, with no other protection but the turban, the symbol of their faith."[218]

Recently, on August 26, 2015, in an op-ed piece in the *San Antonio Express-News*, retired Brig. Gen. Jeffery Kendall (US Army) wrote,

> During World War I, Sikhs serving in the British army were known as the "Black Lions" due to their ferocity on the battlefield, with Sikh regiments receiving more Victoria Crosses per capita than members of any other British unit. Three Sikh Americans have successfully served in the U.S. military with their articles of faith in recent years. In one case, Maj. Kamaljeet Singh Kalsi was deployed as a doctor to a forward location in Afghanistan and received the Bronze Star for saving countless lives while wearing his turban, his beard and his Army combat uniform.
>
> Additionally, claims of an inability to adhere to health and hygiene practices or wear gas masks are without merit. Special operations forces have worn long hair, mustaches and beards under combat field conditions for nearly 15 years. Since 2007, more than 100,000 soldiers have been granted approval for facial hair profiles. Bearded soldiers, like Maj. Kalsi, have

---

[217] http://www.nytimes.com/1992/02/14/opinion/l-for-sikh-independence-367792.html

[218] General Sir Frank Messervy, KCI, KBE, CB, DSO. From the foreword of Colonel F. T. Birdwood OBE, the Sikh Regiment in the Second World War

successfully worn gas masks, and women entering basic training are no longer required to cut their hair short.[219]

Sikh soldiers fought most honorably alongside all other soldiers with the Allies between World War I and II to protect freedom, liberty, democratic values, and all those ideals which America cherishes. It is, indeed, sad that Americans are clueless and have forgotten the unbelievable sacrifices made by these brave men of faith. Instead of honoring the Sikhs, we seem to have an acute case of amnesia.

The first Sikh soldier to serve in the US Army was Bhagat Singh Thind, enlisting in July 1918 and happily accepted by the US Armed Forces with his turban and beard intact. He went on to get his doctorate from the University of California, Berkley, CA.

Bhagat Singh Thind in US army uniform, 1918

---

[219] http://www.mysanantonio.com/opinion/commentary/article/Remove-military-uniform-barrier-for-Sikhs-6467316.php

Mrs. Vivian Thind and Dr. Bhagat Singh Thind, 1958

This is not simply based on their physical prowess but genuine and fierce loyalty toward any freedom- and liberty-loving government wherever they reside. Universal brotherhood, love for all, equality, freedom, and liberty are enshrined in the Sikh scripture, and these fundamental postulates play a very big part in the mental makeup of all Sikhs. It is also not in the makeup of the followers of the Sikh faith to interfere in the faith of others.

"In early 2002, a turbaned Sikh New York City police officer, Amrik Singh Rathour, was terminated for refusing to remove his turban only a few weeks after he had completed training to be inducted into the NYPD."[220]

---

[220] *Civil Rights in Wartime: The Post-9/11 Sikh Experience*, Dawinder Singh Sidhu & Neha Singh Gohil (2009) [214P] ISBN:978-0-7546-7553-2 www.ashgate.com; Page 92

NYPD Police Officers Jasjit Singh Jaggi and
Amrik Singh Rathour at a press conference in NY City

This is a case of a NY City police officer who was asked to remove his turban and be clean-shaven after being hired by the city. It took a legal battle to get Amrik reinstated and get an apology.[221] These constant battles for employment sap the vitality out of any able-bodied Sikh American job applicant.

Prior to 1960, there were simply very few Sikhs in America, but for the last fifty years, there are nearly 500,000 of them, and it is only recently a very small minority have started to file employment-based discrimination lawsuits. For decades, Sikhs have swallowed the very bitter pill of blatant employment discrimination and ended up being self-employed in the thousands by buying farms, owning small businesses, working in factories/mills, driving taxis and trucks without putting up a legal fight.

Then, there is the religious edict for the right to bear arms in the Sikh faith akin to the second amendment in our (US) Constitution. 'Til 1981–1982, the US Armed Forces allowed Sikh Americans to join with their religiously

---

[221] http://www.prnewswire.com/news-releases/sikh-officer-to-file-discrimination-suit-against-nypd-over-no-turbans-policy-74525802.html

mandated turban. Unfortunately, the population of Sikh Americans was small. Then suddenly, Ronald Reagan passed a new law that stated "the no headgear policy," which effectively shut out any practicing Sikh American from being able to serve in the US Armed Forces.

One of the last ones to enter and serve before the law got passed was Col. (Retd) Dr. G. B. Singh, US Army Medical Core. After a gap of nearly 27 years, Tejdeep Singh Rattan (a dentist), Kamaljeet Singh Kalsi (a doctor), and Simarjeet Singh Lamba (an engineer) were allowed to join but through a special provision and a waiver.[222] Captain Rattan is still serving and planning to make a career out of it. Major Kalsi served two tours in Afghanistan with distinction and awarded the Bronze Star.[223] Corporal Lamba continues to serve and may go through Officer Training School since he holds a Master's in Engineering.[224] But the law has not been changed yet, and the "turban ceiling" continues to exist while the committed Sikh Americans continue their long-drawn battle to be freely accommodated in order to serve their country with pride.

Both officers have been making the rounds during their time off across the nation, attending various venues within the community at Gurdwaras, addressing the Sikh American youth, trying to inspire and empower them, and on Capitol Hill so that others may follow in their footsteps and give back to their nation.

---

[222] http://www.army.mil/article/36339/sikh-soldiers-allowed-to-serve-retain-their-articles-of-faith

[223] http://americanturban.com/2011/12/07/us-army-soldier-kamaljeet-singh-awarded-bronze-star/

[224] http://www.dailymail.co.uk/news/article-1328634/Simranpreet-Lamba-First-Sikh-US-army-soldier-nearly-3-decades.html

Iknoor Singh

On June 15, 2015, Iknoor Singh, a sophomore at Hofstra University in Long Island, New York, won a landmark decision to be able to serve in the Reserve Officers Training Corps (ROTC) without cutting his hair, shaving his beard, and removing his turban, all religiously mandated.[225] It is to be seen how the US Army reacts to this ruling by the honorable US District Court Judge Amy Berman Jackson in Washington, DC, on June 13, 2015. Her ruling stated, "It is difficult to see how accommodating plaintiff's religious exercise would do greater damage to the Army's compelling interests in uniformity, discipline, credibility, unit cohesion, and training than the tens of thousands of medical shaving profiles the Army has already granted."

Finally, some semblance of sanity has prevailed, and the law will help open the door for every practicing (religious) Sikh American to serve their country with pride rather than being discriminated against while trying to defend their country.

---

[225] http://abcnews.go.com/US/wireStory/sikh-college-student-wins-battle-army-hair-turban-31782248

The mere fact that there are even a handful of turbaned Sikh Americans serving in the US Armed Forces is a wonderful thing because by highlighting this, it not only inspires young Sikh Americans to work toward eventually joining and serving the US Armed Forces but also makes them comfortable in their faith. The flipside being that the larger majority sees the unique Sikh concept of "Saint-Soldier" in action and slowly understands what the turban of the Sikhs actually stands for!

STRATEGIES FOR REDUCING PREJUDICE AND DISCRIMINATION

CONTROLLED PROCESSING

Prejudice and stereotyping fall under the purview of social phycology. How one gauges and responds to others who are different from one's own group can fall under two subcategories—namely, automatic information processing and controlled information processing. Automatic and controlled information processing come into play often in everyday life, including when we are confronted with stereotypes and strangers.

According to Natalie Boyd,

> Psychologist Patricia Devine first pointed out that when people come into contact with others from another group, they automatically process the information of the others as stereotypes. For example, when Leo, a black man, and Alex, a white woman, first meet, they both automatically think of stereotypes. Leo automatically assumes that Alex is nurturing, and Alex assumes Leo is a good basketball player.
>
> However, that first automatic processing is not the end of the story. Non-prejudiced people overwrite the automatic processing with controlled processing. Maybe Leo thinks to himself, "I don't really know Alex, so maybe she's not nurturing. I'll just have to wait and see." And maybe Alex thinks to herself, "Who knows if Leo even likes basketball? Maybe he prefers croquet."

When they are both able to let go of their early, automatic processing stereotypes and instead relied on their controlled processing, they are able to move beyond stereotypes. If they are not able to engage in controlled information processing, though, their stereotypes turn into prejudice.[226]

In other words, do not prejudge anyone without pausing and thinking. First, give every first contact some thought, then engage in some form of communication—only then can you figure out to some extent what and who the other person is made up of, without any preconceived assumptions.

My father was wise in more ways than I can count and sometimes did things which went against the societal norms. Every school teaches children that they should never speak to strangers and all for the right reasons. But my father always taught us that it is okay to speak to strangers. He said the only way to make friends is to talk to strangers, and only then can all barriers be broken in order to have good relationships with others who hopefully and eventually become friends. Without being preachy, the Sikh scripture states, "I have no enemy, I see no strangers, I consider all my friends."[227] In my own neighborhood, everybody knows my brother and me because we have always got out of our comfort zone and not just said hello to anybody and everybody walking by but tried to strike a conversation with the old and young. This has made my immediate neighborhood a wonderful place to live without the feeling that we are being judged for being different-looking.

RECATEGORIZATION

The key here is moving "others" closer to "us." When the majority, which happens to be politically, economically, and socially stronger any other person(s) who are in the minority, then the minority will always feel like the outsider unless and until included in the majority's social group at

---

[226] http://study.com/academy/lesson/stereotypes-and-automatic-controlle d-information-processing.html Natalie Boyd, MA
[227] Guru Granth Sahib, the Sikh scripture

the minimum. For example, at a Scouting camp, if there are three small groups of children working independent of each other, the minute there is a presumed issue from the other group, arguments and more serious issues can ensue. But if there is a bigger goal, such as a fun movie, which requires everyone's participation or no one is allowed to go, suddenly all those who has minor issues with each other make an extra effort to work with each other in order to make something good happen for "all," even though there may be a slightly selfish motive.[228]

IMPROVING GROUP CONTACT

Group contact has shown in hundreds of studies to positively improve perceptions of each other. One great example is "bussing," which had its problems, but when the law of the land was changed to make it happen over time, when "whites" were bussed to "black" school schools and vice versa, the preconceived notions did change as the interaction increased with time. As Dr. Charles Stangor puts it, "Busing also improved the educational and occupational achievement of Blacks and increased the desire of Blacks to interact with Whites; for instance, by forming cross-race friendships. Overall, then, the case of desegregating schools in the United States supports the expectation that intergroup contact, at least in the long run, can be successful in changing attitudes."[229] Similarly, if any small group, like the Sikh American children, makes a concentrated effort but with a similar effort being reciprocated by the larger "in" group of European American children, then there is a definite change in the perceptions, making pre-emptive positive change, which only bodes well for society in general.

EMPATHY TRAINING

This is one topic that is talked about, yet there has not been any kind of practical solution which shows concrete results anywhere. "Empathy" is an overrated word because it has been underutilized. In order to put some

[228] http://opentextbc.ca/socialpsychology/chapter/reducing-discrimination/
[229] http://opentextbc.ca/socialpsychology/chapter/reducing-discrimination/

real teeth to "empathy training," it has to become part of the vast spectrum of the school's intrinsic curriculum. Simply holding a class session once a year for an hour or so by teaching kids that they have to become more empathetic to others is not enough! It takes parents years to teach their children good manners, etiquette, honesty, and other qualities in order to be a good citizen as an adult. Similarly, "empathy" has to be taught and inculcated by spending time and repeating it many, many times for it to actually make an impact permanently.

Schools have to design a program around sensitive issues, such as possibly bringing children from the school of the blind, the school of the deaf, children with various disabilities to regular schools on a rotating basis. If a disabled child comes to a regular school once a month for one hour and not only talks about his/her life with the particular disability but answers questions by the peer audience, it will open all children's hearts and create more empathy.

Furthermore, when these children are brought from outside to interact and teach nondisabled children, the nondisabled children must actually role play and try to be in the disabled child's "shoes" for a short while to truly understand what it feels like to be handicapped. Giving presentations and showing movies are good, but for a child to actually understand something, it has to be done with a real life example.

Therefore, to make it even more meaningful, if busloads of normal children actually go to, for example, to the school of the blind and spent a few hours being blindfolded while trying to do all the normal activities the blind child has to do, it would make a world of difference in the empathy level of the normal, nondisabled child. The nondisabled child would certainly understand how hard it is to have physical handicaps and the daily challenges which go with it. This kind of interaction, if made a part of the general curriculum of all schools across the country, would make real and meaningful inroads toward genuine "empathy training," thereby reducing bullying.

For any idea to stick, it takes time and patience, but it definitely requires training and repetition. This type of "empathy training" will not only help reduce bullying but will make all children grow into much better human beings who genuinely feel for others, not simply tolerate others. In my "dictionary," "tolerance" is a bad word. Does that mean that there is a fine line beyond which my tolerance level can be breached and there will be consequences for the other? The right word is "real, genuine respect," and in order to create that, it will require school administrations to find ways around our nation's convoluted laws to start practical empathy training. Let us stop coddling the school children as though they are too delicate to deal with the harsh inequities of physical handicaps, different religious attires, etc., of other children. Just like all children have to deal with death of a sibling, a parent, or an adult close relative, similarly certain out-of-the-box experiments must be done for the improvement of society for a better tomorrow.

HERDING SYNDROME

Anyone that has gone through a Catholic school, a private school, or any boarding school can relate to and understand long-term childhood friendships. For example, when a child enters 5th grade and he/she stays with the same group of 25–50 classmates all the way to 12th grade, the child will know everyone and vice versa. Next, if all the students end up taking the same courses and staying together, the friendships end in lifelong bonds. All this can only happen when all the students stay together without being split up, especially at a crucial time in the high school phase when friendships and bonding is crucial.

The reality today is very different in public schools across America. From kindergarten to 5th grade in most schools, all the students remain physically in the same class with the kids they know as the teachers come to their class and teach them while the students actually remain there without moving out of their classroom. Once children go into middle school and then high school, each child is taking a mix of courses out of a large menu of courses available to the students. Most friendships formed previously get strained because it is rare for any two children to have the same courses at any given time, starting sometimes as early as the 6th grade. Further, the children physically move from classroom to classroom, like college, moving like herds of sheep through the hallways, a perfect setting for bullying. So, this "herding syndrome" setup is not conducive to creating friendships and is much more prone to bullying.

There may not be a perfect solution to this issue! Should the students be kept in the same classroom while the teachers move to those classrooms and teach? First, there will be much less traffic due to hundreds of children rushing through hallways. Secondly, it will decrease bullying by others during that time. And finally, those children will build better, long-lasting friendships which they will cherish as adults.

This is not a simple issue, and much thought must be given by administrators across the nation on the long-term effects and consequences as the flipside of friendship is bullying.

CONCLUSION

There are several suggested solutions for adults, from parents to all sections of the school authorities and the legislators. There is no single solution but a mix of various ones which can and will work if done right. All of them require sustained and diligent effort by all those who want to see all our young ones become bright, productive, upstanding citizens so bullying becomes a thing of the past and not the common norm of today.

CONCLUSION

"Progress is impossible without change,
and those who cannot change their minds cannot change anything."
George Bernard Shaw[230]

Until we all realize that no matter what our religion may be, we are all the same on the inside—blood, bones, etc.—as a society, it is up to us to make the world we live in a place where children of all ethnicities, all religions—Sikh, Muslim, Jews, Buddhist, Baha'i, Christians, or no faith—can go to school and receive an education where there is absolutely no bullying so that all can thrive and rise to be noble citizens of this great country.

The world is changing rapidly. There is no excuse for ignorance, at least in America. The world's knowledge is easily accessible through the computer thanks to the numerous search engines. Ignorance by design can only be detrimental to our own mental health. No school-going middle schooler and beyond can have an excuse that he/she was not taught something, especially something so simple as reading about a geographic area, a little basic history, and about someone's faith, because all that is available a mouse click away.

It is imperative that we all understand and embrace diversity, are multilingual, respect other faiths/cultures along with all the other educational qualifications, are going to go places, and become not only great American

---

[230] http://www.brainyquote.com/quotes/topics/topic_change.html#50jR351M0w WAD2A8.99

citizens but also global citizens. Today, an IT professional has a laptop and travels globally to develop software programs. Business school graduates are working in other countries running great companies. Engineers cannot be locked into any geographic area if we need more energy, like oil! Physicians are being consulted via Skye for years across borders for their expertise. Attorneys are being used for various niche specialties from intellectual law to human rights across borders.

We must accept each other with our differences in appearance or accent or other minor issues. The "us" versus "them" has to stop and be changed to "we" the people as enshrined in our great constitution. Let us stop paying lip service to those words. Instead, let us make a genuine effort to make tomorrow a bully-free world. We need all hands on deck to steer the American ship properly in the changing global community.

We have to empower students, educators, families, and communities with information and tools to prevent bullying. Knowledge of who is a Sikh is a critical component of this process. The recent initiative on Capitol Hill about Sikh American children legitimizes the concerns the Sikh American community has been vociferously stating for a long time, particularly since 9/11.

My survey and the strategies are only the beginning of a long road ahead to resolve bullying.

A culture of inclusion rather than exclusion with respect for diversity must be a part of society's foundation.

BIBLIOGRAPHY

BOOKS

Cunningham, Joseph Davey. *The History of the Sikhs*. Satvic Media Pvt. Ltd. 1849. 1st edition. Print.

DeWolf, K. A. *Bullying: Stop Bullying; Effective Ways To Overcome Bullying In School Permanently: Modern Day Approach To Prevent Bullying Once And For All*. 2014. Print.

Gibson, Margaret. *Accommodation without Assimilation; Sikh Immigrants in an American High School*. Cornell University Press. 1988. Print.

Hirsch, Lee, Cynthia Lowen, and Dina Santorelli. *Bully: An Action Plan for Teachers, Parents, and Communities to Combat the Bullying*. 2012. Print.

Jaijee, Inderjit Singh. *Politics of Genocide: Punjab 1984–1998*. Delhi: Ajanta Publications. 1999. Print.

Jasser, Zuhdi M. *A Battle for the Soul of Islam – An American Muslim's Fight to Save His Faith*. Simon and Schuster. 2012. Print.

Khalsa, Sirinam Singh. *Break the Bully Cycle; Intervention Techniques And Activities To Create A Responsible School Community*. Goodyear Books. 2007. Print.

Mayrock, Aija. *The Survival Guide to Bullying*. 2015. Print.

Mann, Jasbir Singh, and Johal Satnam Singh. *Sikh Gadar Lehar 1907–1918*. Shri Guru Granth Sahib Foundation. 2015. Print.

Moore, Michael. *Fahrenheit 9-11*. Simon and Schuster. 2004. Print.

Olweus, Dan. *Bullying at School: What We Know and What We Can Do.* Wiley Blackwell. 1993. Print.

Samagh, Raghbir Singh. *US Congress on Sikh Struggle for Freedom In India.* International Sikh Organization. 1988. Print.

Sandhu, Ranbir Singh. *Struggle for Justice – the speeches of Sant Jarnail Singh Bindrawale.* Sikh Education and Religious Foundation. 1999. Print.

Sekhon, Awatar Singh. *Murder of Pluralism – Democratic Oppression in South Asia.* Sikh Educational Trust. 2013. Print.

Sekhon, Awatar Singh. *25 Years After 1984 Assault on Durbar Sahib – Laying the Foundation of Khalistan.* London Institute of South Asia. 2009. Print.

Sidhu, Dawinder Singh, and Gohil Neha Singh. *Civil Rights in Wartime – The Post-9/11 Sikh Experience.* www.ashgate.com 2009. Print.

Sidhu, Gurmel Singh. *Another Aspect of the Ghadar Movement: The Struggle for American Citizenship and Property Ownership.* Shri Guru Granth Sahib Foundation. 2015. Print.

Singh, Harbans. *The Heritage of the Sikhs.* Manohar Publishers and Distributors. 1983. Print.

Singh, Patwant. *The Sikhs.* Rupa Publications 1999. Print.

Singh, Sangat. *Sikhs in History.* Uncommon Books. 1999. Print.

Singh, Trilochan. *The Turban and the Sword of the Sikhs – Essence of Sikhism.* Chattar Singh and Jiwan Singh. 2001. Print.

ARTICLES

Nijher, Kirpal Singh. "Who is a Sikh?" 2014. Print.

Sandhu, Ranbir Singh. "Sikhs in America." 2004. Print.

Singh, Beant. "Why I am not an Indian." 2006. Web.

Singh, Kavneet. "Book Review of *Civil Rights in Wartime – The Post 9-11 Sikh Experience.*" 2013. Print.

WEBSITES

www.thirdsikhgenocide.org

www.americansikhcouncil.org

www.worldsikhcouncil.org

www.sikhtoons.com

www.sikhcoalition.org

www.saldef.org

www.bullying.org

http://www.state.nj.us/education/holocaust/resources/

http://www.state.nj.us/education/

http://www.bullyingstatistics.org/content/bullying-and-suicide.html

CONFERENCES

"Sustained Sikh Genocide 1984–1998" held at Princeton University, New Jersey, on February 7, 2015.

GLOSSARY

1. Gurdwara: a Sikh house of congregational prayer, erroneously called a "temple" by some.

2. Darbar Sahib: the holiest of holy, house of prayer, also known as "Harmandar Sahib." Incorrectly and erroneously called the Golden Temple.

3. Kande Da Phaul: the formal Sikh initiation ceremony, also known as "amrit sanchar," after which a Sikh is becomes part of the "Khalsa"—a sovereign fraternity of equals (men and women) who are formally committed to upholding all the righteous values of the faith.

4. Rehat Maryada: the Sikh moral code of conduct applies to anyone who claims to be a Sikh. The Sikh code of conduct was formulated by the Sikh collective starting on March 15, 1927, and finally completed and approved on February 3, 1945.

5. Punjab: the homeland of the Sikhs which was an independent kingdom formed in 1799 but annexed by the British on March 29, 1849 to British India.

6. India: modern India never existed as there were over 550 separate kingdoms and countries which were slowly tied together by the canny British over a period of two and a half centuries, and then a made-up name by the British was applied to the whole. Later, in 1947, British India was split in two based on religious lines by partition, forming modern India and modern Pakistan.

7.   Turban: dastaar, dastar, pagri, patka, keski, dumala are all names for the Sikh turban and some of its styles.

8.   Sikh: meaning student or learner in Punjabi. Sikh, Sikhs, or Sikh American is alternatively applicable in this book.

9.   Hindu: the word "Hindu" does not exist in any of the umpteen religious Hindu texts anywhere. It is the British who helped coalesce a myriad of faiths under the umbrella of Brahmanical Hinduism and labeled all the divergent beliefs within British-controlled "pre-India" as Hinduism, even though the actual name is "Sanatan Dharma."

10. Maharaja Ranjit Singh: the first sovereign emperor of the Sikh kingdom, which started in 1764 and became a kingdom formally in 1799, while he ruled 'til his passing away in 1839, though the Sikh kingdom existed 'til 1849.

APPENDIX A

1. Have you ever been bullied in school?
   - Yes
   - No

2. How many times have you reported to your teacher, administration, or the principal about being bullied last year?
   - Never
   - Once in a while
   - Sometimes
   - Frequently
   - Very frequently

3. How often do you get bullied in school?
   - Never
   - Once in a while
   - Sometimes
   - Frequently
   - Very frequently

4. How long have you lived in the United States?
   - Born and raised in the US
   - 1 to 5 years
   - 6 to 10 years
   - 11 or more years

5. What is your gender?
   - Male
   - Female

6. How old are you?
   - 5 to 10
   - 11 to 14
   - 15 to 18
   - Other

7a. What is the name of your school? (Names of schools were removed for privacy.)

7b. What is the name of your town and state? (Names of towns and states were removed for privacy.)

7c. What is your zip code? (Zip codes were removed for privacy.)

8. When taking part in school activities, how often have you been excluded due to your appearance—patka/dastar/turban/long braids?
   - Never
   - Once
   - One to five times
   - Many times
   - Grown a thick skin—don't care

9. How regularly do you get called out in the hallways?
   - Almost never
   - Once in a while
   - Sometimes
   - Frequently
   - Almost all the time

10. Where have you been bullied? (Check all those that apply; therefore, there are overlaps.)
   - In the classroom
   - On the bus
   - Outside of school

- On the internet
- Recess/bathroom
- Other

11. Why do you think you get bullied?
    - My dastar/patka/keski
    - My hair
    - My kara
    - Other

12. How motivated are you to confront the bullies?
    - Not at all motivated or afraid
    - Slightly motivated
    - Somewhat motivated
    - Quite motivated
    - Extremely motivated

13. Have you taken up a martial art in order to protect yourself from bullies?
    - No/never
    - Considering it
    - Did do it for a while
    - Have been doing it regularly
    - Have a 1st–4th degree black belt

14. Have you taken up public speaking in or out of the school by participating in, for example, Sikh Youth Symposium, Hemkunt Speech Symposium, Model UN, National Speech and Debate Association?
    - Not at all
    - Tried it and stopped
    - Do it sometimes
    - Do it regularly and has helped face bullies somewhat
    - Do it and has helped face bullies easily

15. Have you ever felt discriminated against by a teacher or staff?
    - Not at all
    - A little bit
    - Somewhat
    - Quite a bit
    - A tremendous amount

16. Why do you think students get bullied? (Check all that apply; therefore, there are overlaps.)
    - Race/skin color
    - Gender
    - Religion (turban/dastar/patka)
    - Shyness
    - Disability
    - Physical appearance (how one looks)

17. Do you have any suggested solutions to stop bullying toward Sikhs?
    - School administration to teach Sikh heritage to the entire school.
    - School teachers to be educated and understanding toward Sikhs.
    - School administration to be able to punish bullies quickly and firmly.
    - School administration, teachers, and other school adults to be more inclusive of kids like me and not simply pay lip service with the claim of being unbiased.
    - State law changed so that the school administration can implement all the above in order for me to be "bully free" in school, hopefully.

18. Optional comments and suggestions.

1. Have you ever been bullied in school?

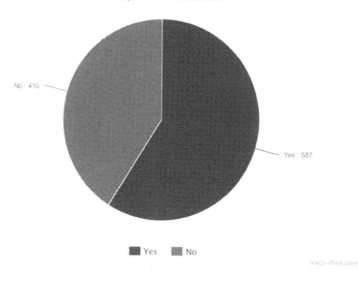

2. How many times have you reported to your teacher, administration or the principal about being bullied last year?

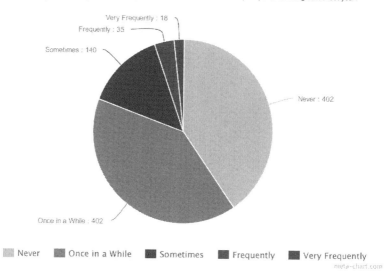

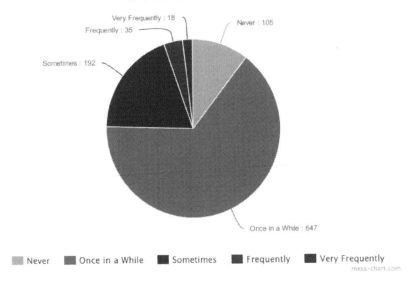

3. How often do you get bullied in school?

Very Frequently : 18
Frequently : 35
Never : 105
Sometimes : 192
Once in a While : 647

Never   Once in a While   Sometimes   Frequently   Very Frequently

meta-chart.com

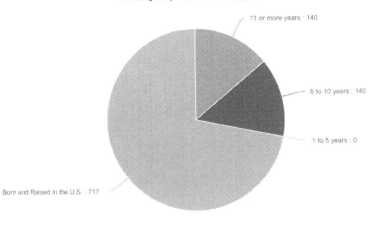

4. How long have you lived in the United States?

11 or more years : 140
6 to 10 years : 140
1 to 5 years : 0
Born and Raised in the U.S. : 717

11 or more years   6 to 10 years   1 to 5 years   Born and Raised in the U.S.

meta-chart.com

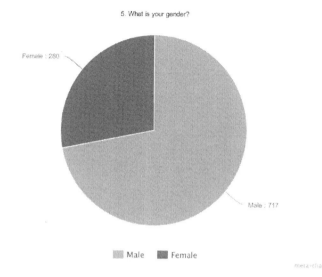

5. What is your gender?

Female : 280

Male : 717

Male   Female

meta-chart.com

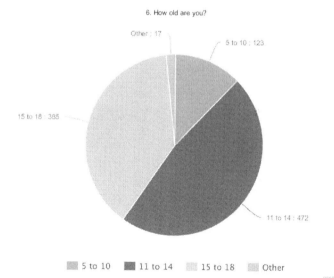

6. How old are you?

Other : 17

5 to 10 : 123

15 to 18 : 385

11 to 14 : 472

5 to 10   11 to 14   15 to 18   Other

meta-chart.com

7. When taking part in school activities, how often have you been excluded due to your appearance – patka/dastar/turban/long braids?

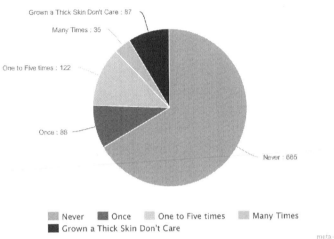

8. How regularly do you get called out in the hallways?

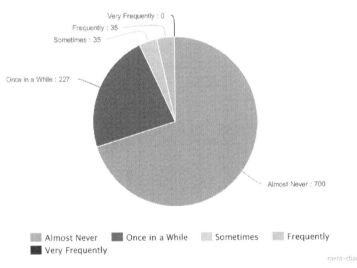

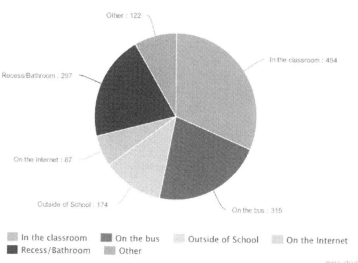

9. Where have you been bullied?

Other : 122

In the classroom : 454

Recess/Bathroom : 297

On the Internet : 87

Outside of School : 174

On the bus : 315

In the classroom   On the bus   Outside of School   On the Internet
Recess/Bathroom   Other

meta-chart.com

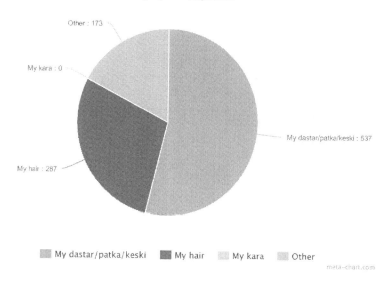

10. Why do you think you get bullied?

Other : 173

My kara : 0

My dastar/patka/keski : 537

My hair : 287

My dastar/patka/keski   My hair   My kara   Other

meta-chart.com

11. How motivated are you to confront the bullies?

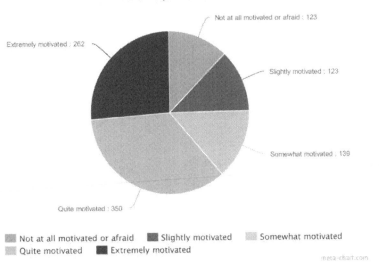

Not at all motivated or afraid : 123

Extremely motivated : 262

Slightly motivated : 123

Somewhat motivated : 139

Quite motivated : 350

Not at all motivated or afraid   Slightly motivated   Somewhat motivated
Quite motivated   Extremely motivated

12. Have you taken up a martial art in order to protect yourself from bullies?

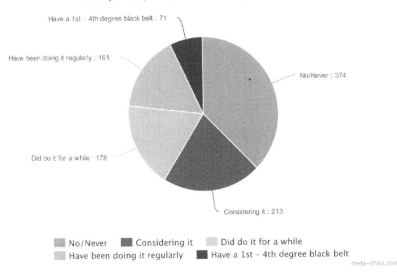

Have a 1st – 4th degree black belt : 71

Have been doing it regularly : 161

No/Never : 374

Did do it for a while : 178

Considering it : 213

No/Never   Considering it   Did do it for a while
Have been doing it regularly   Have a 1st – 4th degree black belt

13. Have you taken up public speaking in or out of the school by participating in; for example, Sikh Youth Symposium, Hemkunt Speech Symposium, Model UN, National Speech and Debate Association?

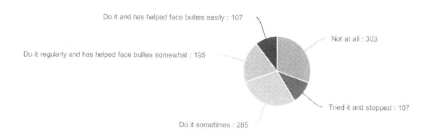

Do it and has helped face bullies easily : 107

Not at all : 303

Do it regularly and has helped face bullies somewhat : 195

Tried it and stopped : 107

Do it sometimes : 285

Not at all   Tried it and stopped   Do it sometimes
Do it regularly and has helped face bullies somewhat
Do it and has helped face bullies easily

meta-chart.com

14. Have you ever felt discriminated against by a teacher or staff?

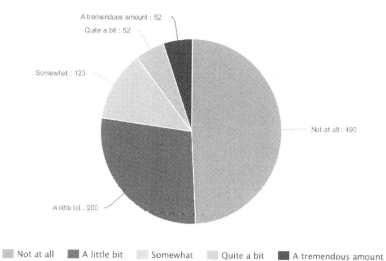

A tremendous amount : 52
Quite a bit : 52
Somewhat : 123
Not at all : 490
A little bit : 200

Not at all   A little bit   Somewhat   Quite a bit   A tremendous amount

meta-chart.com

15. Why do you think students get bullied?(Check all that apply).

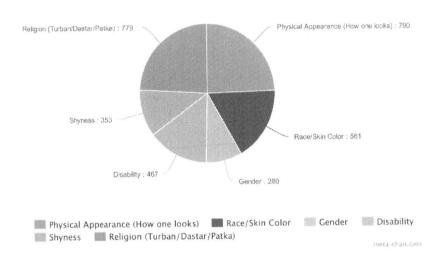

Religion (Turban/Dastar/Patka) : 779

Physical Appearance (How one looks) : 790

Shyness : 353

Race/Skin Color : 561

Disability : 467

Gender : 280

- Physical Appearance (How one looks) - Race/Skin Color - Gender - Disability
- Shyness - Religion (Turban/Dastar/Patka)

meta-chart.com

16. Do you have any suggested solutions to stop bullying towards Sikhs?(Check all that apply).

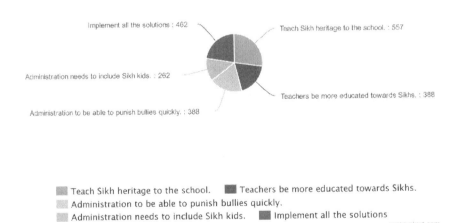

Implement all the solutions : 462

Teach Sikh heritage to the school. : 557

Administration needs to include Sikh kids. : 262

Administration to be able to punish bullies quickly. : 388

Teachers be more educated towards Sikhs. : 388

- Teach Sikh heritage to the school. - Teachers be more educated towards Sikhs.
- Administration to be able to punish bullies quickly.
- Administration needs to include Sikh kids. - Implement all the solutions

meta-chart.com

238

APPENDIX B

List of questions for child psychiatrists and child psychologists in reference to bullying trauma

1. How does bullying affect children in the 6–15-year age group in general?

2. How does taunting about a child's heritage or religion laced with racial epithets affect children?

3. Does severe and continuous bullying cause PTSD (post-traumatic stress disorder)?

4. If severe bullying does cause PTSD, how does one diagnose it?

5. What are the solutions for this kind of PTSD?

6. For severe physical bullying, such as forcefully removing a child's turban, cutting a child's hair, burning a child's turban, and/or beating a child senseless (all the above are actual instances), what should be the steps taken by the child (and his/her parents) in order to get justice?

7. If an elementary or even a middle school child is ostracized through shunning by a teacher, how and what can a child do when he/she cannot even understand clearly the reason why the adult is bullying?

8. Should "empathy training" be mandatory to create better-conditioned children, and if so, what are the steps to do it?

9. For Sikh American kids who (the male and female) do wear religiously mandated headgear, what kinds of solutions do you suggest?

10. What can the school administration do to help this particular situation?

11. What can the Sikh American child do to fend off bullies, especially when the bullying is done by a group away from the gaze of any adults (e.g., inside the bathroom, locker room, gym)?

INDEX

Made in the USA
Middletown, DE
05 September 2019